KV-193-515

Introduction

Places

Culture

Travel Tips

▷ **Grand' Place (p20)**
The focal point of the old
city, with its stunning
array of baroque facades.

△ **Galeries St Hubert
(p48)** Browse round
the high-class shops in
Europe's first glass-
covered mall.

▷ **Horta Museum
(p70)** The beautiful
house of the Belgian
master of art nouveau.

▽ **Sablon Squares
(p35)** Two elegant
squares in the Upper City.

▷ **Historical and
Modern Art Museums
(p26)** Collections from
Breughel to Magritte.

▷ **Brussels Park
(p31)** The Parliament,
Royal Palace and the city
centre's relaxing park.

△ **Cinquantenaire Park (p59)** Three excellent museums in the European Quarter.

▷ **St Michael's Cathedral (p48)** Brussels' principal place of worship took over 600 years to complete.

▽ **Palace of Justice (p37)** This monumental building towers over the colourful Marolles quarter.

△ **Ilôt Sacré (p47)** Make your way here for mussels and chips.

The Capital of Europe

Mention Brussels, and what will most immediately spring to mind is the increasingly important role that the city plays in the lives and destinies of millions of European citizens. But this is no accident of history, for Brussels, today's capital designate of Europe, has long played a role in developments on the continent. In the days when the Low Countries were in French hands, then in Spanish, then in Austrian, Brussels was always the chosen capital of 'the Netherlands'. Even after becoming the capital of the independent Kingdom of Belgium in 1830, the city maintained a strongly European identity.

> **Where the sights are**
> Many, but by no means all, of Brussels' attractions lie within the pentagonal circuit of boulevards that comprise the inner ring road, and some of the finest are within strolling distance of the Grand' Place. This simplifies sightseeing by dividing the city into three nested zones: around the Grand' Place; inside the inner ring road, and beyond the inner ring road.

A Thriving City

The latter half of the 20th century saw Brussels consolidate its position as capital of Europe, first becoming, in 1958, headquarters of the European Economic Community (EEC) and the European Atomic Energy Community (EURATOM). A year before these two bodies, and the European Coal and Steel Community, merged to become the European Community in 1967, the city became home to the headquarters of the North Atlantic Treaty Organisation (NATO), which moved here from France. Due to the concentration of important European institutions in Brussels, the city now ranks third world-wide, behind Paris and London, as a centre for congresses.

Although the poets and thinkers, artists and merchants it once attracted have now been largely superseded by the planners of the European Union and NATO, Brussels remains a thriving place, where citizens not only of Europe but of the world can feel at home. As the capital of Europe, the profile presented by the city evolves from year to year. In addition to its venerable and noteworthy sights dating from past centuries, including its magnificent market square, the Grand' Place, Brussels also presents an increasingly modern face to visitors as ever more new office blocks are erected to meet the demands of the city's emergent role.

Opposite: the Town Hall on the Grand' Place
Below: the modern face of Brussels: office blocks

Porte de Hal: one of the few remnants of the medieval city walls

LOCATION AND SIZE

Brussels, the capital of Belgium, is located almost in the centre of the country. The northwest boundary of the country is a coastline of 67km (42 miles). Belgium is bordered to the north by the Netherlands, to the east by Germany, to the southeast by Luxembourg and to the south and southwest by France.

The city centre is contained within a mere 3,292ha (8,134 acres) while metropolitan Brussels sprawls over 16,000ha (39,535 acres). Because parts of Brussels are situated on hills along the Senne valley, the altitude of the city ranges from 15–100m (49–328ft) above sea level. For this reason, a distinction is made between the lower city, which includes the Old Town, and the upper city which affords a lovely panorama of the lower-lying neighbourhoods. The downtown area, enclosed by a boulevard ring which follows the path of the former city wall, is now largely a commercial and business centre as the residential population moved out to the suburbs, although some quarters have recently been revitalised by an influx of younger people moving back into the city centre. It is here that the offices of the Belgian government and parliament are found, while most of the EU offices are located further east around the Rond-Point Schuman.

EARLY HISTORY

According to legend, Brussels was founded in the 6th century by Saint Géry on an island in the Senne river, on a site that had been inhabited by the Romans and later by the Franks. It was first documented in AD966 in a chronicle of Emperor Otto I which referred to it as Bruocsella ('Settlement in the Marshes'), the seat of many counts from the region. Several islands in the Senne, located at the site of today's city centre, were declared military outposts and in 977 a small wooden fort was constructed on one of them. In 979 Charles, Duke of Lorraine made it his residence. For this reason, 979 is regarded as the year in which the city was officially founded.

The real development of the city began in the 11th century when the later-to-be Duke of Brabant settled on the Coudenberg, the site of today's Place Royale and surrounding streets. Brussels' location on an important trade route of the time, between Cologne and Bruges, ensured prosperity throughout the 12th and 13th century. The city's burgeoning wealth soon began to express itself in the form of fine buildings. Brussels grew to become one of the major towns in the duchy of Brabant. Its economy was largely based on the manufacture of luxury fabrics, which made their way to fairs in Paris, Venice and elsewhere. Business and municipal matters were almost exclusively controlled by a handful of wealthy merchant dynasties who had grown rich and powerful from the cloth trade. Their abuse of power led to a number of popular uprisings during medieval times.

However, it was not until 1531, when the Habsburg Emperor Charles V declared Brussels the capital of his Low Countries dominions, and the later completion of the Willebroek Canal, which connected the city to Antwerp and the sea, that it acquired a status equal to the other wealthy towns of Flanders. Artists and academics settled in Brussels, and rebellions against Spanish Habsburg rule started here. In 1695, the attempt by Louis XIV of France to capture the city reduced

Below: Counts Egmont and Hornes were executed in 1568 for their rebellion against Spanish rule
Bottom: medieval life in Belgium, as depicted in Bruges Town Hall

the lower town to rubble and ashes. Brussels remained as capital during the periods of Spanish, Austrian and French rule, but the city's economy did not really start to flourish in a modern sense until after the 1830 revolution against Dutch rule which left Belgium free and independent.

Below: King Leopold I pursued his imperial ambitions in Africa
Bottom: the Cinquantenaire Arch, erected to celebrate 50 years of nationhood

AN INDEPENDENT NATION

With independence came phenomenal economic growth but also social, political and religious conflicts. Tensions were high between Catholics and liberals, and between Flemings (Dutch-speaking Belgians in the north) and Walloons (French-speaking Belgians in the south). Although Brussels was nominally bilingual, French was increasingly dominant in business and state administration. The Flemings campaigned with increasing indignation for greater use of their language in the universities and law courts.

Throughout the 19th century and particularly during the reign of Leopold II (1865–1909), industrial expansion and imperial exploitation in the Congo brought great prosperity to Brussels. There was a flurry of construction, with magnificent mansions and commercial buildings rising up along the wide avenues and boulevards.

This was matched by an explosion of artistic achievement in the capital. Painters including

James Ensor, Félicien Rops and Fernand Khnopff came together in the Groupe des XX in 1883. Brussels was also a major centre of Art Nouveau architecture under the leadership of Victor Horta and Paul Hankar.

THE TWO WORLD WARS

Belgium's historic vulnerability to invasion was displayed again in August 1914, when Kaiser Wilhelm's German armies occupied Brussels. The capital put up heroic passive resistance, and when the Germans were defeated, Belgium expressed its new-found sense of national unity in the introduction of universal suffrage, the right to strike, and a Flemish university. In the 1930s there emerged in Brussels, as in other European capitals, new fascist groups drawing on social discontent and primitive chauvinism. These grim times offered a fertile breeding ground for a flight into the Surrealist art of René Magritte and Paul Delvaux, and the inspired comic-strip escapism of Hergé's Tintin.

Then came World War II and another German occupation. The Nazi invaders found a few collaborators to prepare Belgium for integration into the Reich, and King Leopold III caused controversy with his passive acceptance of the invasion.

Leopold abdicated in 1951 in favour of his son Baudouin. He proved to be an immensely popular monarch and is generally credited with holding the nation together when conflict between Flemings and Walloons threatened to tear it apart. Baudouin died in 1993 and, since he and Queen Fabiola had no children, was succeeded by his brother, Albert II.

ECONOMY

The post-war years, particularly the 1960s, were a time of prosperity and optimism for Belgium, symbolised by the Atomium, the city's famous landmark, and a massive road-building project, which has enabled Brussels to become an important crossroads not just for Belgium, but for the

To see or not
Getting around by Brussels' Metro is quick and efficient, but you won't see much (if you exclude the works of modern art that grace many Metro stations). Brussels is not such a big city, so unless you're really pushed for time, you'd do better to go by tram or by bus, in that order – and in the central zone around the Grand' Place, on foot.

Flying the flag on National Day, 21 July

Double speak

Brussels is officially bi-lingual, and street names and the names of museums and all manner of other visitor attractions are in both French and Dutch. The reality though is that French speakers are in the majority and this is the language that most foreign visitors will attempt if they want to communicate. (Flemish is a variant of Dutch, with differences in pronunciation, vocabulary and expressions.) And so most Brussels names in this book are given in French. In those places outside the city in Flanders, place names are given in Dutch, the official language.

whole of Europe. The Belgian capital looks somewhat like a spider in a net, serving as the hub for routes leading into the city from Liège, Namur, Charleroi, Mons, Ghent and Antwerp. These spokes are all linked by a huge motorway, known as the Ring, which encircles Brussels.

Several international railway lines also lead through Brussels, making it a central junction for one of the world's most densely concentrated railway systems. These lines play an important role in linking the United Kingdom and Germany as well as France and the Netherlands. The 6-line underground rail system (the Metro) was built in 1952 to link the former terminal stations in the northern and southern parts of the city.

Although water transport in Brussels is fairly insignificant for tourism, the city's canal routes play a major role in the national economy. The Charleroi Canal links the capital with the industrial regions in the south of Belgium, while the Willebroek Canal provides access to the Brussels inland harbour on the Scheldt river, leading to Antwerp and the open sea.

As the Belgian financial capital, Brussels is the seat of the national bank and an important stock exchange. Despite the growth in service industries, the city remains a major manufacturing centre. The textile industry, with its production of wool and upholstery materials and Brussels lace, has a long tradition. Modern industries encompass the metal, electrical, chemical and pharmaceutical sectors. Brussels also produces fine food and an excellent array of unusual beers, which are reaching an ever-wider international market.

Lace-making, a skill practised in Belgium for centuries

POPULATION AND LANGUAGE

Situated only a few kilometres north of the linguistic border between Flemings in the north and Walloons in the south, Brussels is officially bilingual. The visitor will immediately notice that signs and street names, as well as all the city districts, are labelled in both Dutch and French. Speakers of the French language, however, are definitely in the majority.

The city centre of Brussels, strictly defined, has only about 145,000 inhabitants. However, 19 semi-autonomous communities are joined with the centre to form Brussels Capital Region, with a population of just over one million (the population of Belgium is 10.2 million). Almost one-third of Brussels' inhabitants are foreigners, giving the city a distinctly cosmopolitan air.

In addition to the long-established Congolese community, a substantial Islamic population originating from North Africa and Turkey has more recently developed. The ethnic mix is diverse and dynamic enough to rival any capital city.

CULTURE CAPITAL

Brussels' role as the cultural centre of Belgium is evidenced by the location here of the Royal Academy, founded in 1772, the Free University (1834) and the Polytechnic Institute (1873), a number of art academies and institutes of higher learning and the Albert I Library. In addtion, nearly 100 museums, covering a vast range of subjects, from art, history and architecture through to beer, puppets and human anatomy, testify to the city's status as a cultural focal point. Among the many theatres and cultural centres offering performances in several languages, the Théâtre National de la Monnaie is the most important.

Below: Brussels is a multi-ethnic society
Bottom: Théâtre National de la Monnaie

HISTORICAL HIGHLIGHTS

966 The first mention of Brussels.

Around 1100 The first fortification walls are built in Brussels.

1379–83 After Brussels' occupation by the troops of the Count of Flanders, a new, 6-km (4-mile) long city wall with 74 towers and six gates is constructed. The line of the wall, shaped like a coat of arms, is almost identical to that of the inner boulevard ring surrounding the city centre today.

1402 Construction of the Town Hall begins in the market place.

1421 A popular uprising leads to a fairer system of government, with local powers divided between the patrician families and the emergent guilds of craftsmen and other workers.

1430–77 Philip the Good becomes ruler of Brabant and Brussels. The Burgundian period sees Brussels become the favourite residential city of the Duke of Burgundy in the Low Countries, which constitute a rich centre of art and culture.

1455 The city has a population of 40,000.

1521 The Humanist Desiderius Erasmus of Rotterdam resides in Anderlecht.

1522 The treaty between Charles V and his brother Ferdinand, dividing the Habsburg empire between the German and the Spanish lines, is signed in Brussels. Two Lutheran preachers are burned at the stake in Brussels; their martyrdom strengthens the forces of the Reformation in the city.

1531 Emperor Charles V chooses Brussels as the capital of the Habsburg Netherlands. Mary of Hungary and Margaret of Parma also later reside here.

1561 Completion of today's Sea Canal, named the Willebroek Canal, which links Brussels to the Scheldt and thus to the North Sea; thereafter, three large harbour basins are dug in the northern part of the city.

1566 The first revolt of the Netherlands against its Spanish sovereign breaks out.

1568 The Counts Egmont and Hoorn, leaders of the resistance movement, are executed in the market place.

1579-85 After the southern provinces of the Low Countries (which included modern-day Belgium) separate from the northern provinces (now the Netherlands), Brussels returns to the Roman Catholic fold.

1598–1633 The reign of Archduke Albert and Isabella. The Counter-Reformation leaves its mark on the city landscape with the construction of a series of fine churches in the Italian-Flemish baroque style.

1695 The French, under Marshal Villeroi, bombard Brussels; hundreds of buildings are destroyed by fire. The numerous French wars against Spain and Austria have already adversely affected Brussels, hampering its prosperity, but after this catastrophe new guild halls are built, the architectural landmarks now surrounding the market place, or Grand' Place.

1794 Following the Brabant revolt against the government of Austrian Emperor Joseph II, the Belgian principalities are annexed to France. The French revolutionary government names Brussels as capital of the Dyle Departement.

1815 Napoleon is defeated just outside Brussels, at Waterloo.

1815–30 Brussels and The Hague alternate as the seat of the monarchy after the Congress of Vienna orders the merging of the territory of today's Belgium and the Netherlands, creating the United Kingdom of the Netherlands.

1830 The Belgian revolution erupts in Brussels. Belgium declares its independence and is chosen as the capital.

1831 Leopold of Saxe-Coburg arrives with great ceremony in Brussels and becomes the first Belgian king, taking the name Leopold I. Brussels becomes the seat of the Belgian monarchy.

1846 The Galeries Royales Saint-Hubert *(see page 48)* is built near the Brussels market place. It is the first glass-covered shopping arcade in Europe. Seven neighbouring communities are incorporated into Brussels, forming an Agglomération which is later joined by 11 other bordering communities.

1897 Brussels World Exhibition in Cinquantenaire Museum and Exhibition Palace.

1914–18 World War I. Adolphe Max, the burgomaster of Brussels, acquires fame for his resistance to the German occupying forces.

1935 World Exhibition in Brussels/Heysel.

May 1940 Brussels falls to the invading German armyand is subjected to harsh terms of occupation. Leopold III is interned in Laeken Castle. Germany tries to divide the nation by supporting partisans of Flemish autonomy.

September 1944 The city is liberated by the British and the legitimate Belgian government returns to its capital from London.

1951 Leopold III abdicates in favour of his son Baudouin.

1952 Construction of an underground railway connection between the North and South stations. Construction of the Gare Centrale to the east of the Grand' Place.

1958 International World Exhibition at Heysel fair grounds. The fair's landmark is the Atomium, and the event helps to boost the weakened post-war economy. Brussels becomes the seat of the European Economic Community (EEC).

1967 NATO headquarters moves from France to Belgium.

1989 In the reorganisation of the Belgian state, Brussels becomes the Capital Region, alongside Flanders and Wallonia.

1993 King Baudouin dies and is succeeded by his brother Albert.

1995 The provinces of Flemish Brabant and Walloon Brabant are created from the old province of Brabant, giving Belgium a total of ten provinces.

2000 Brussels is one of the European Capitals of Culture.

2002 The euro replaces the Belgian franc.

2003 Belgium amends its controversial 1993 war crimes law which had seen actions brought against US President George W Bush amonst others and had led to threats to boycott Brussels as an international meeting place.

2004 Paedophile Marc Dutroux is sentenced to life imprisonment. The far-right Vlaams Blok is disbanded and quickly reforms as the Vlaams Belang (Flemish Interest).

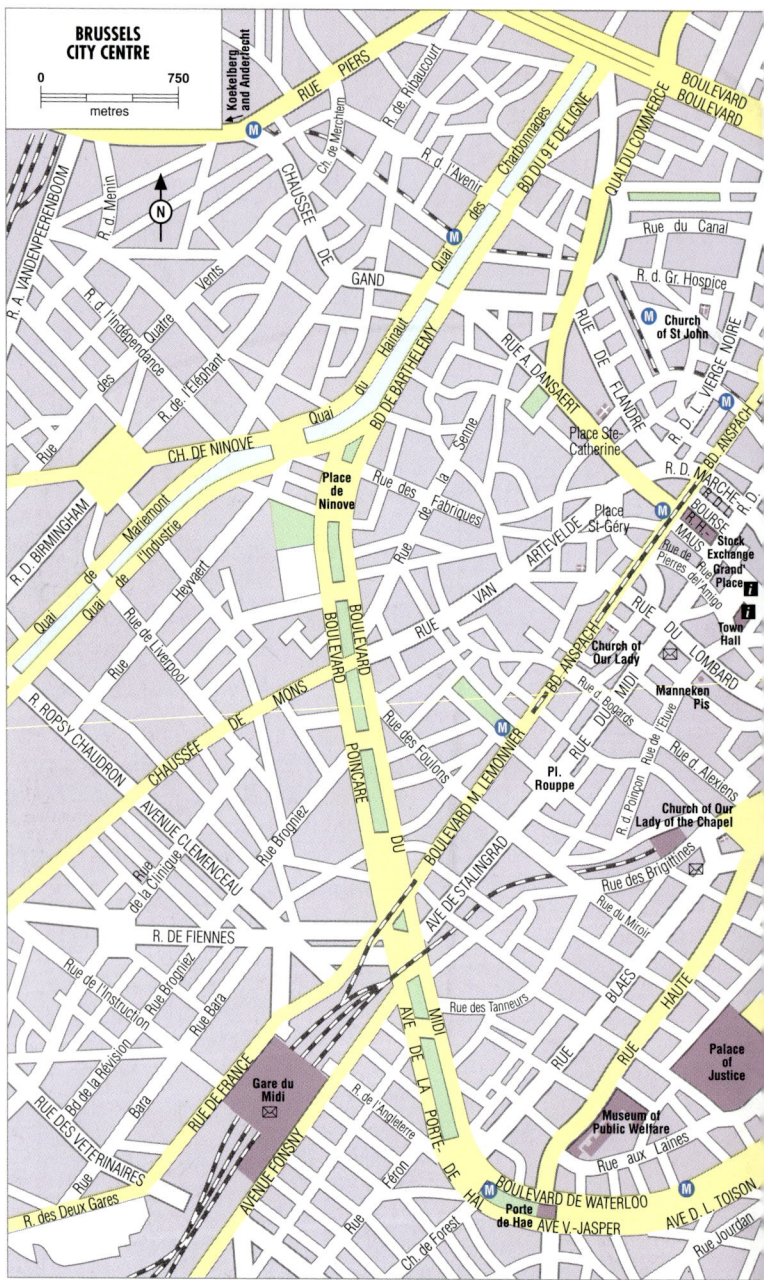

BRUSSELS CITY CENTRE

0   750

metres

Koekelberg and Anderlecht

N

RUE PIERS

R. de Ribaucourt

BOULEVARD

BOULEVARD

QUAI DU COMMERCE

Ch. de Merchten

CHAUSSÉE DE GAND

Charbonnages

BD DU 9 E DE LIGNE

R. d'Avenir

des

Rue du Canal

R. d. Gr. Hospice

Church of St John

R. D. L. VIERGE NOIRE

R. DE FLANDRE

BD ANSPACH

R. D. MARCHÉ

R. A. VANDENPEEREBOOM

R. d. Menin

Vents

Quatre

R. d' l'Independance

des

R. de l'Éléphant

Quai du Hainaut

BD DE BARTHÉLEMY

la Senne

RUE A. DANSAERT

Place Ste-Catherine

CH. DE NINOVE

Quai

Rue

Place de Ninove

Rue des Fabriques

de la

Place St-Géry

ARTEVELDE

Place St-Géry

BOURSE

Stock Exchange

R. D. MAUS

Rue de R. amigo

Pierres der'Amigo

Grand Place

R. D. BIRMINGHAM

Marienont

de l'Industrie

Heyvaert

Rue de Liverpool

BOULEVARD

BOULEVARD POINCARÉ

RUE VAN

Rue

RUE DU LOMBARD

Town Hall

Church of Our Lady

Manneken Pis

Rue d. Bogards

DU MIDI

Rue de l'Étuve

Rue d' Alexiens

R. ROPSY CHAUDRON

CHAUSSÉE DE MONS

Quai

Rue

Rue des Foulons

BOULEVARD M. LEMONNIER

Pl. Rouppe

R. d. Poinçon

Church of Our Lady of the Chapel

AVENUE CLÉMENCEAU

Rue de la Clinique

Rue Broigniez

DU

AVE DE STALINGRAD

Rue des Brigittines

Rue du Miroir

R. DE FIENNES

Rue de l'instruction

Rue Broigniez

Rue Bara

MIDI

Rue des Tanneurs

BLAES

RUE

HAUTE

RUE DES VÉTÉRINAIRES

Bd. de la Revision

Bara

RUE DE FRANCE

Gare du Midi

R. de l'Angleterre

AVE DE LA PORTE DE HAL

Palace of Justice

Museum of Public Welfare

Rue aux Laines

R. des Deux Gares

AVENUE FONSNY

Féron

Rue

Ch. de Forest

BOULEVARD DE WATERLOO

Porte de Hae

AVE V. JASPER

AVE D. L. TOISON

Rue Jourdan

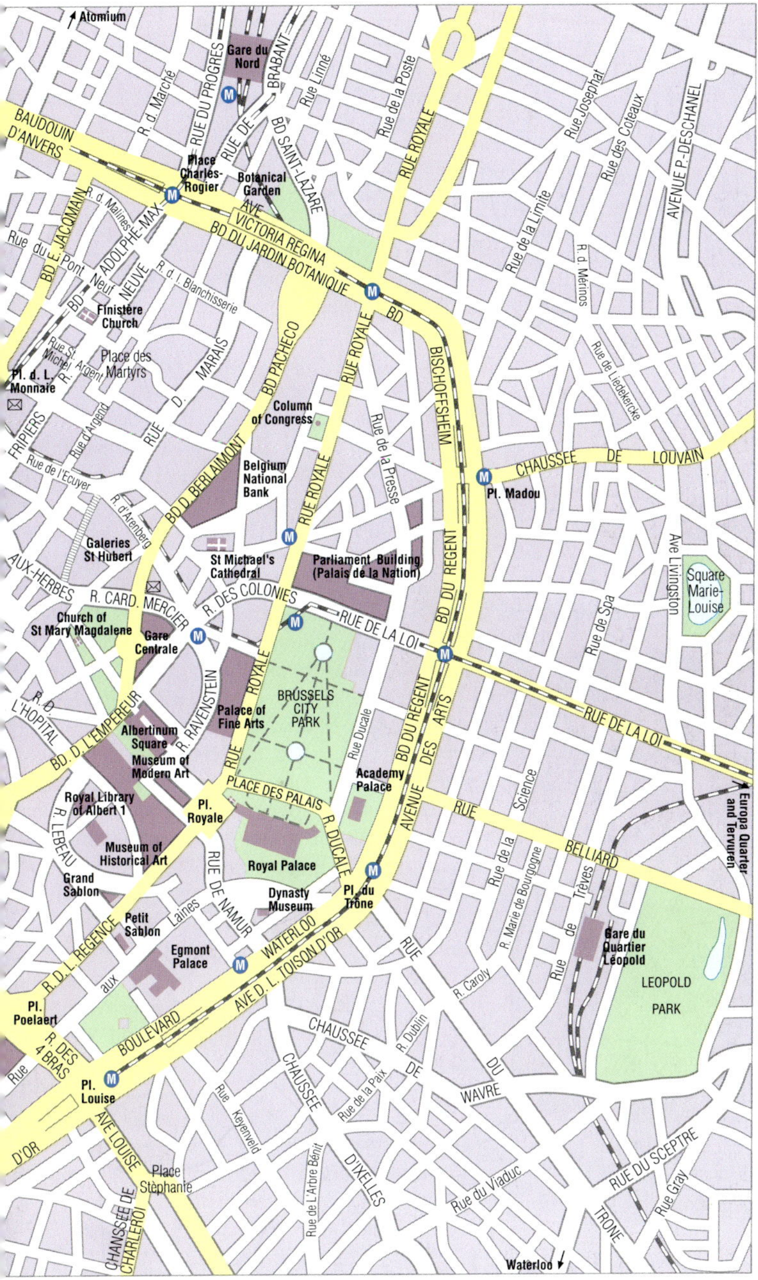
Atomium
Gare du Nord
Place Charles-Rogier
Botanical Garden
BAUDOUIN D'ANVERS
AVE VICTORIA REGINA
BD DU JARDIN BOTANIQUE
RUE DU PROGRES
RUE DE BRABANT
BD SAINT-LAZARE
Rue Linné
Rue de la Poste
RUE ROYALE
Rue Josephat
Rue des Coteaux
AVENUE P.-DESCHANEL
Rue de la Limite
R. d. Mérinos
R. d. Marché
R. d. Malines
BD E. JACQMAIN
BD ADOLPHE-MAX
Rue du Pont Neuf
BD NEUVE
R. d. l. Blanchisserie
Finistère Church
Place des Martyrs
Rue St. Michel
R. Argent
Pl. d. L. Monnaie
RUE D. MARAIS
BD PACHECO
Column of Congress
BD BISCHOFFSHEIM
Rue de Liedekercke
Rue de la Presse
CHAUSSEE DE LOUVAIN
Pl. Madou
FRIPIERS
Rue d'Argent
Rue de l'Ecuyer
BD D. BERLAIMONT
Belgium National Bank
R. d'Arenberg
Galeries St Hubert
St Michael's Cathedral
Parliament Building (Palais de la Nation)
BD DU REGENT
Ave Livingston
Square Marie-Louise
AUX-HERBES
R. CARD. MERCIER
R. DES COLONIES
RUE DE LA LOI
Church of St Mary Magdalene
Gare Centrale
Rue de Spa
R. D. L'HOPITAL
BD. D. L'EMPEREUR
R. RAVENSTEIN
Palace of Fine Arts
BRUSSELS CITY PARK
Rue Ducale
AVENUE DES ARTS
Albertinum Square
Museum of Modern Art
Royal Library of Albert 1
Pl. Royale
PLACE DES PALAIS
R. DUCALE
Academy Palace
RUE BELLIARD
Rue de la Science
R. LEBEAU
Museum of Historical Art
RUE DE NAMUR
Royal Palace
R. Marie de Bourgogne
Rue de Trèves
Europa Quarter and Tervuren
Grand Sablon
Petit Sablon
Laines
Dynasty Museum
Pl. du Trone
RUE DE
Gare du Quartier Léopold
R. D. L. REGENCE
Egmont Palace
WATERLOO
AVE D. L. TOISON D'OR
R. Caroly
LEOPOLD PARK
Rue aux
Pl. Poelaert
BOULEVARD
CHAUSSEE DE WAVRE
R. Dublin
R. DES 4 BRAS
Pl. Louise
CHAUSSEE D'IXELLES
Rue de la Paix
Rue Keyenveld
D'OR
AVE LOUISE
Rue de L'Arbre Bénit
Rue du Viaduc
RUE DU SCEPTRE
Rue Gray
TRONE
Place Stéphanie
CHAUSSEE DE CHARLEROI
Waterloo

Map on pages 18–19

Fatal mistake

According to a spurious local legend, the architect of the Town Hall committed suicide by jumping off the spire when he noticed that the tower had not been placed at the centre of the facade.

Weekly flower market on the Grand' Place

1: The Grand' Place

Town Hall – guild halls – King's House – City Museum – House of the Dukes of Brabant – House of the Swan – Belgian Brewers' Museum

As a matter of course every visitor to this city is drawn to the centre, to the Town Hall Square, known in French as ★★★ **Grand' Place** and in Flemish as Grote Markt.

This is, without a doubt, not only the focal point of the city but also a superb example of a medieval city centre. It is, quite simply, one of the most lovely squares in the world. The harmony of today's baroque facades is due to the solidarity shown by the guilds during the period following the bombardment and almost total destruction of the square by French troops in 1695. Not only did they agree to rebuild the square in its former style, they also completed the work in five years.

In former times the Grand' Place was the commercial, political and cultural centre of Brussels, a role which it has, over time, unfortunately sacrificed. Today, although the main offices of the industrial giants, housed in modern glass structures, are still located inside the inner boulevard ring, they are scattered throughout the entire downtown area. The same is true for the government offices. And so today the Grand' Place is dominated by crowds of tourists from around the world. Arriving mainly in groups, they listen fleetingly to the tour guide's brief description of the square before hurrying on to the next sight. Those few who manage to linger a bit longer here, retreating from the tumult perhaps to the refuge of one of the coffee-houses, might be able to call to the mind's eye an image of what this square once was, of life before the hustle and bustle of modern times.

THE TOWN HALL

The most prominent building is the ★★ **Town Hall** (Hôtel de Ville; guided tours in English: Apr–Sept Tues and Wed 3.15pm, Sun 10.45am and 12.15pm; Oct–Mar Tues and Wed 3.15pm;

admission fee), one of the best-preserved secular structures from the Gothic period. The larger portion of the building, to the left, was built from 1402 to 1404. The smaller section, on the right, was added in the years after 1444, hence the asymmetry. The tower, adorned with a statue of St Michael, the patron saint of Brussels, was completed in 1454 and restored in 1997. The top of the tower (400 steps up) offers a spectacular view of the city. The rear portion of the complex was rebuilt after the French attack but was not finally completed until the 18th century. The facade of the Town Hall is decorated with numerous statues, which include several interesting examples of 14th- and 15th-century Brussels sculpture.

THE BRUSSELS TAPESTRIES

In addition to the facade, interesting attractions are the two fountains (from 1715) in the courtyard, symbolising the Meuse and Scheldt rivers, as well as several large rooms inside the building where the so-called Brussels Tapestries are housed. Originally appointed in neoclassical style, the main Council Chamber was redesigned in 1868 as a Gothic Hall. Tapestries adorning the walls depict the city's principal traditional crafts and the guilds which practised them. The wall hangings were created between 1875–81 in

Star Attractions
- **Grand' Place**
- **Town Hall**

Below: café life on the Grand' Place
Bottom: Town Hall facade

Map
on pages
18–19

Place of Execution

In 1568, Count Egmont and Count Hoorn, the celebrated leaders of the revolt against the Catholic policies pursued by Philip II within the Spanish Netherlands, were held in the King's House before their execution on the Grand' Place.

Mechelen. Former presidents of the municipal council are represented as gilt bronze statues in front of the columns, and the windows illustrate the coats of arms of noble Brussels families.

It is possible to walk around the entire Town Hall complex following the Rue Charles Buls (further along this road is the famous statue of Manneken-Pis, *see Route 3, page 33*), the Rue de l'Amigo (rear facade) and the Rue de la Tête d'Or, ending up back at the Grand' Place, right next to the Town Hall.

GABLED GUILD HALLS

Seven old ★**guild halls** are crowded closely together along the square. Some of their historic names, listed here, have been changed over the centuries and do not always correspond to the names displayed today. House No 7 is the Haberdashers' House, sometimes also called the Fox House owing to the figure above the door. No 6 is the Mariners' House (1696), its gable aptly designed as a ship's stern. The next house, No 5, is the Archers' House (1691), a survivor of the bombardment, also known as the House of the She-Wolf, based on the figure of the Capitoline she-wolf with Remus and Romulus. Note the gilt Phoenix on the gable. House No 4 is the Joiners' and Coopers' House (built in 1644, restored

The King's House, now the City Museum

in 1697). At No 3 is the House of the Tallow Makers. Finally, at No 1/2 is the Bakers' House (1697) featuring a bust of the Spanish king Charles II, now a popular tavern with a remarkable interior, Le Roy d'Espagne.

Star Attraction
•City Museum

THE HISTORY OF BRUSSELS

The facade of the building opposite the Town Hall, on the other end of the square, is divided into three sectors. In the centre is the King's House, flanked on either side by more guild halls. The **King's House** (Maison du Roi), originally called the Bread House (Broodhuis) when it served as the bakers' guild hall, was reconstructed in its present form between 1873 and 1895, in an imitation of its original 16th-century style.

In the past the King's House has been the seat of various courts and a prison, but today it is home to the ★★ **City Museum** (Musée de la Ville; open Tues–Fri 10am–5pm, Sat–Sun 11am–5pm; admission fee), which was opened in 1887. Aside from the magnificent building itself, the museum's many attractions include the collection of 26 paintings donated to the city by an Englishman, John Waterloo Wilson. These works include the *Allegory of the United Provinces* by Verkolie, *Still Life with Food* by Willem Claesz Heda and *Portrait of a Clergyman*, attributed to Josse van Cleve.

The museum's collection also presents a first-class chronicle of the city, with statues of the prophets originally displayed in the Town Hall (late 14th-century), two Brussels altarpieces from the late 15th and early 16th century, four 16th-century Brussels tapestries including *The Legend of Notre-Dame-du-Sablon* (attributed to Barend van Orley), the painting *Wedding Procession* by Pieter Brueghel the Elder as well as the most complete collection of Brussels ceramics, dating from 1710–1845.

There is also a series of fascinating maps and pictures that recall the era when the River Senne ran through the centre of the city.

The museum has a separate section called the

Guild houses on the Grand' Place

Map
on pages
18–19

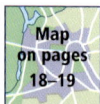

Celebrated houses

Adjacent to the King's House are the Painters' House (Nos 27–26), the Tailors' House (No 25), now home to another famous tavern called La Chaloupe d'Or (the Golden Galleon), and the House of the Old City Scales (No 24).

Wardrobe of Manneken-Pis (Garderobe de Manneken-Pis; *see page 33*). It houses a kitch collection of over 500 different costumes which have been donated to the city since the 18th century for this renowned figure, Brussels' oldest citizen and a city landmark.

KARL MARX LIVED HERE

On either side of the King's House are small alleys leading to the Rue du Marché-aux-Herbes, location of the Belgian Tourist Office (No 63) where multilingual staff are available to help.

At the other side of the Rue de la Colline is the **House of the Dukes of Brabant**, dating from 1698. This building forms one end of the rectangular market place. Consisting of six former guild halls, it was named for the busts of the dukes which adorn the capitals of the Ionic columns along the facade. At the end of this row, the Rue de Chapeliers leads off the square. Across that street is the Town Hall facade which houses, in addition to the Town Hall itself and the Brussels tourist office, more guild halls, including: No 12, the House of the Three Colours (1699); No 11, the House of the Rose (1702), No 10, the Brewers' House (with a gilt equestrian statue of Charles of Lorraine); No 9, the **House of the Swan** (1698), the former guild hall of the butchers (once the home of Karl Marx and now one of the city's most elegant restaurants), and No 8, the Star House, originally constructed in the 13th century and rebuilt several times, most recently in 1897.

House of the Swan, once the butchers' guild hall

A NATIONAL PASSTIME

The Brewers' House is the site of the ★ **Belgian Brewers' Museum** (Musée des Brasseurs Belges; open Apr–Nov daily 10am–5pm, closed Tues Jan–June and Sept–Nov; Dec–Mar Sat–Sun noon–5pm; admission fee). An insight into an important part of the national identity, it features both an old brewery displaying traditional equipment, and a modern one using the latest techniques. Beside the brewery is a lively bar.

2: Royal Brussels

Chapel of St Mary Magdalene – Albertinum – Museums of Historical and Modern Art – Place Royale – Royal Palace – Palace of Fine Arts

Statue in Albertinum Square

Because of the Grand' Place's important role and its central location – it is situated close to the Central Station as well as to three underground stations – all of the walking tours through the downtown area *(Routes 2–6)* begin and end at this point. Leave the square via the Rue de la Colline and go southeast towards the large museums and the Royal Palace. To the right, the Rue de la Madeleine leads along a small park to the **Chapel of St Mary Magdalene** (La Chapelle de la Madeleine) ❶, a Gothic prayer chapel dating from the 15th century, renovated in 1956. At that time the small baroque chapel of St Anna was moved here from the Rue de la Montagne. The Rue de la Madeleine, continuing alongside the park, leads to **Albertinum Square** (Place de

Map on page 25

Albert's memorial
The Albertinum, in its present form, was erected from 1954–65 as a memorial to King Albert I. It houses several libraries and museums and the collections together comprise over five million volumes.

l'Albertine) ❷, bordered by the Mont des Arts, the Palace of Congress (Palais des Congrès) and the huge complex of the Albertinum. This structure extends southeast where it is joined by the Museum of Historical Art, which in turn extends to the Rue de la Régence.

In the **Royal Library of Albert I** (Bibliothèque Royale Albert Ier; open to cardholders only) ❸ the working rooms of the poet Emile Verhaeren and the playwright Michiel de Ghelderode have been reconstructed. The adjacent Book Museum (Musée du Livre) houses valuable printed works and manuscripts, donated by the heirs of prominent families. The complex also features the history of books in the Printing Museum and an audio-visual archive of French and Belgian literature.

MUSEUM OF HISTORICAL ART

The southeastern section (entrance on Rue de la Régence) houses the ★★ **Museum of Historical Art** (Musée d'Art Ancien) ❹ (open Tues, Wed and Fri 9.30am–5pm, Thur 9.30am–8pm, Sat–Sun 10am–5pm; admission fee). This was built in neoclassical style from 1875–81 based on plans by Balat. The four granite columns of the facade are crowned by bronze busts of Rubens, Jean Bologne and Jan van Ruysbroek. To the side and above are two bronze groups, *The Crowning of*

The Census of Belgium by Breughel hangs in the Museum of Historical Art

the Fine Arts (P de Vigne) and *The Inspiration of Art* (Van der Stappen). The Royal Museum of Historical Art was reopened in 1887 in the Palais Balat after originally being housed in the buildings of the former court of Charles of Lorraine.

Star Attraction
• **Museum of Historical Art**

FLEMISH MASTERPIECES

The museum's superb collection of paintings is largely from the Flemish school of art, which includes works by such renowned artists as Brueghel the Elder, Rubens and Van Dyck, to name just a few.

The museum contains works from the 15th–18th centuries, with an especially rare example of the painting of the pre-Van Eyck period, *Scenes from the Life of the Holy Virgin*, one of the oldest known examples of painting on wood. Additionally, the museum houses three works of the Master of Flémalle including a *Prophecy*, six paintings by Rogier van der Weyden (1400–64) including the *Pietà* and the *Man with the Arrow*, two large paintings by Hugo van der Goes (1440–82), the two famous pictures of the four *Pictures of Righteousness* by Dirk Bouts (1415–75), paintings by Hans Memling (1440–94), including *The Martyrdom of St Sebastian*, *The Holy Virgin with the Milk Soup* by Gerard David (1460–1523), *Crucifixion with Donor* and the triptych *The Temptation of St Anthony* by Hieronymus Bosch (1460–1516). The love that Pieter Brueghel the Elder (1520–69) had for his native landscapes becomes evident in a series of important paintings.

Another masterpiece by Brueghel, housed in the department of 16th–17th-century works, is part of the collection donated by Delporte. It is *A Winter Landscape with Ice Skaters and Bird Traps*. The Rubens Hall within the 17th-century department contains fabulous baroque creations by this master such as *The Assumption of the Virgin Mary*, *The Adoration of the Magi*, *The Martyrdom of St Livinus*, *Ascending Calvary* and the portrait of Hélène Fourment, the 16-year-old bride of Rubens.

Below: the Museum of Historical Art
Bottom: Massacre of the Innocents *by Dirk Bouts*

Map on page 25

La Mort de Marat *by Jacques-Louis David immortalises one of the martrys of the French Revolution*

The Jordaens Hall houses *The Allegory of Fertility* and, among the works of Van Dyck, the wonderful *Portrait of a Genoese Lady and Her Daughter*. This hall also contains works of the French, Dutch and Italian schools and several major works by Lucas Cranach the Elder. Next to the museum is the open air sculpture garden, a peaceful retreat in the city centre.

MUSEUM OF MODERN ART

The Rue de la Régence at this point crosses Route 3. Just a few hundred metres away is the church of Notre-Dame-des-Victoires-au-Sablon *(see page 36)*. At the corner of Place Royale is the entrance to the ★★ **Museum of Modern Art** (Musée d'Art Moderne) ❺ (open Tues–Sun 10am–5pm; admission fee). The eight floors of subterranean rooms provide a huge exhibition space, supplied with sufficient natural lighting via a light shaft.

Of particular interest here are paintings, drawings and sculptures of the 19th- and 20th-century French and Belgian schools. The most important works of modern sculpture include works by artists such as Constantin Meunier, Souply, Rodin and César. The 19th-century paintings and the Paul Maas collection are representative of the Belgian and foreign schools: Classicism, Romanticism and Symbolism, Realism, Impressionism and Pointillism. Some of the most important works are those by the artists Alfred and Joseph Stevens and Louis Dubois *(Les Cigognes)*. The Belgian Impressionists exhibited here include Emil Claus, Anna Boch and Isidore Verheyden. The French influence is evidenced in Theo van Rysselberghe's *Portrait of Madame Charles Maus*.

BELGIAN SURREALISTS

Several important works by French painters can be seen here, including three paintings by Jacques-Louis David *(La Mort de Marat)* and the famous study *Apollon vainqueur du serpent python* by Delacroix. There are also several works by French artists such as Gauguin, Seurat and Signac. Henry Moore, Andy Warhol, Keith Haring and Francis Bacon are also represented. Other paintings of note hanging in the museum are the Fauvist paintings of Rik Wouters', including *Le Flûtiste*, Evenepoe's *Henriette au Grand Chapeau*, and the expressionist Permeke's *The Engaged Couple* and the Ostend native James Ensor's *Les Masques Singuliers*.

The Surrealists are represented by Paul Delvaux *(Pygmalion)* and René Magritte *(L'Empire des Lumières)*. Masterpieces such as *Nu à Contrejour* by Pierre Bonnard and *La Tentation de Saint Antoine* by Salvador Dalí are on display.

Star Attraction
• **Museum of Modern Art**

Below: keyboard in the Museum of Musical Instruments
Bottom: young Belgians at a royal parade

MUSEUM OF MUSICAL INSTRUMENTS

Just before Place Royale, on Rue Montagne de la Cour, you'll see the elegant Magasins Old England building, home to the ★★ **Museum of Musical Instruments** (Musée des Instruments de Musique) ❻ (open Tues–Fri 9.30am–5pm; Sat–Sun 10am–5pm; admission fee), a fascinating collection of over 6,000 rare and beautiful musical instruments from around the world dating from the Bronze Age to the 20th century, including several creations by the Belgian Adolphe Sax, inventor of the saxophone. As you approach each instrument, headphones activated by sensors play music of the period.

Map on page 25

Mostly museums

A little way past the Museum of Modern Art and just off Place Royale is Place du Musée. Walking into this tranquil square is like stepping into another world. It is surrounded by the graceful museum complex, formerly the palace of Charles of Lorraine.

ROYAL BRUSSELS

The ★ **Place Royale** ❼ was built in the 18th century by Barnabé Guimard. Its classical architecture honours Charles of Lorraine, under whose orders many of the city's elegant buildings were constructed. Numerous mansions line the square, including that of Baron d'Arconati Visconti, later owned by the family of the Counts of Flanders. In the middle of the square is a statue of Godfrey of Bouillon, the leader of the first crusade. From the square there is a panoramic view over the Lower City. Also on the square is the church of Saint-Jacques-sur-Coudenberg, a graceful neoclassical structure, built from 1776–85 and inspired by a Roman temple.

The route now leaves the Place Royale towards the Place des Palais, located between the Royal Palace and the Brussels Park. Next stop on the tour is the **Dynasty Museum** (Musée de la Dynastie) ❽ (open Apr–Sept Tues–Sun 10am–6pm; Oct–Mar Tues–Sun 10am–5pm; admission fee) located at Place des Palais 7. The museum houses a wealth of information on the Belgian royal family, dating from 1830 to the present. Within the museum is the King Baudouin Memorial, dedicated to the much-loved monarch who died in 1993, and the Archaeological Site of the Coudenberg, the remains the medieval palace built on this site. Also along this route is the

A flag flying above the Royal Palace indicates that the King is in residence

Palace of the Academies (Le Palais des Académies). Built in 1823–9 in Italian Renaissance style, it was designed as the residence of the Prince of Orange. In 1876 it became the headquarters of the Belgian Royal Academy.

The ★ **Royal Palace** (Palais du Roi) ❾ (open 3rd week July–late Sept Tues–Sun 10.30am–4.30pm; free) was constructed under Leopold II, in the style of Louis XVI, during the second quarter of the 19th century. A copper statue of Leopold II (by Thomas Vincotte) is located behind the palace, which was built on the site of the former palace of the Duke of Brabant which burned down in 1731. That palace, known as the Brussels Court, was the residence of Philip the Good and Charles V. The new one, built by Van der Straeten, was renovated and expanded in 1904–12. The King only occupies this palace for a few days every year; the royal family's principal private residence is now the Laeken Royal Palace (*see page 54*).

BRUSSELS' CONCERT HALL

This tour continues on the other side of Rue Royale, to the **Palace of Fine Arts** (Palais des Beaux-Arts) ❿. Known now by its new, trendy name, Bozar, this complex extends all the way to Rue Ravenstein, where you'll find the entrance. Baron Victor Horta, the father of Belgian art nouveau, is the architect of the Palace of Fine Arts, built from 1921–8. With its great halls for exhibitions, banquets and concerts, it is a focal point of Brussels' cultural life. Adjacent to the palace is Ravenstein House, the only remaining mansion in Brussels dating from the era of the Burgundian monarchy.

The ★ **Brussels Film Museum** (Musée du Cinéma) is on Rue Baron Horta No 9, between Rue Royale and Rue Ravenstein. The museum shows old film classics daily from 5.30pm.

The return route to the Grand' Place leads over the Mont des Arts, across the Boulevard l'Empereur, along the Rue de l'Infante Isabella and past the Chapel of St Mary Magdalene again.

Below: statue of crusader Godfrey of Bouillon on Place Royale
Bottom: the church of St Jacques sur Coudenberg

R. A. DANSAERT
R. STE-CATHERINE
R. D. L. VIERGE NOIRE
BD ANSPACH
R. NEUVE
Rue du Marais
R. D. FRIPIERS
Rue de l'Ecuyer
Belgium National Bank
Rue des Chartreux
Stock Exchange
R. D. L. BOURSE
R. D. MARCHE- A- HERBES
R. H. MAUS
St Nicholas
Galeries St Hubert
R. VAN ARTEVELDE
Pte. R. D. Bouchers
BD D. BERLAIMONT
Rue des Pierres
Notre-Dame-aux-Riches-Claires
Grand' Place
Rue de l'Amigo
Town Hall
R. CARD. MERCIER
Church of Our Dear Lady
Gare Centrale
Church of St Mary Magdalene
R. DU LOMBARD
Rue de la Violette
BD D. L'IMPERATRICE
11
R. de Chêne
Rue d. Bogards
R. de l'Etuve
RUE DU MIDI
12
BD D. L'HOPITAL
Albertinum Square
BOULEVARD M. LEMONNIER
R. d. Alexiens
R. de Villers
R. d. l'Escalier
Pl. Rouppe
Museum of Modern Art
BD DE L'EMPEREUR
R. LEBEAU
Royal Library of Albert 1
14
R. d. Rollebeek
AVE DE STALINGRAD
R. d. Poinçon
13
Museum of Historical Art
15
Rue des Brigittines
R. D. SABLONS
16
R. DE LA REGENCE
Rue du Miroir
RUE BLAES
RUE HAUTE
Rue des Tanneurs
17
R. D. L. REGENCE
18
Rue des Minimes
Rue aux Laines
Pl. Poelaert
Pl. du Jeu-de-Balle
R. DES 4 BRAS
19
BOULEVARD DE WATERLOO
Pl. Louise
21
RUE
AVE D. L. TOISON D'OR
AVENUE LOUISE
Rue aux Laines
BOULEVARD DE WATERLOO
20
AVE DE L. PORTE DE HAL
AVE HENRI- JASPER
Rue Jourdan
N
ROUTE 3
0
500
metres

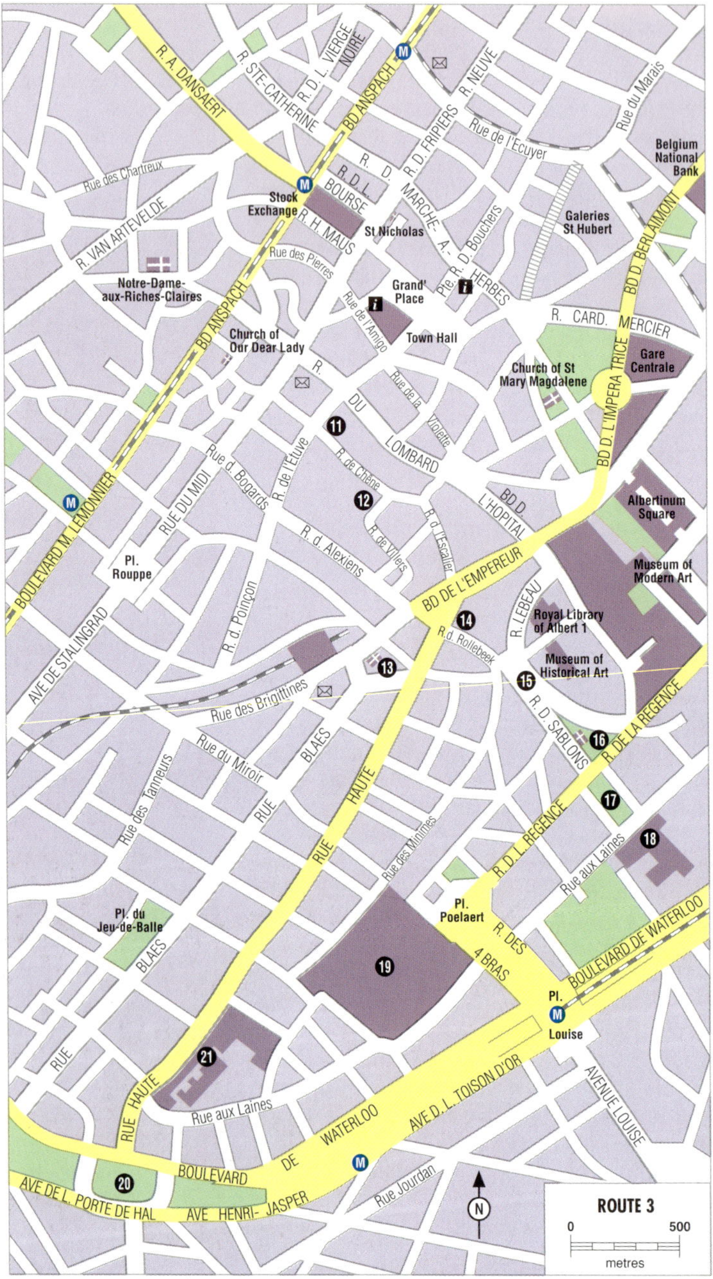

3: Sablon Squares

Manneken-Pis – Church of Our Lady of the Chapel (Notre-Dame-de-la-Chapelle) – Grand- and Petit-Sablon Squares – Palace of Justice – Porte de Hal – Anneessens Tower

Map on page 32

This route leaves the Grand' Place from beside the Town Hall along the Rue Charles Buls in a southerly direction towards the Porte de Hal. Not far from the Town Hall, at the corner of Rue de l'Etuve (the continuation of Rue Charles Buls) and Rue du Chêne is the famous, but disappointingly small, landmark of Brussels, the ★**Manneken-Pis** ⓫. This boy embodies the rebellious spirit of the Brussels people. The bronze statue was created in the 17th century by the Belgian sculptor Jérôme Duquesnoy.

Many legends surround the figure. It is said that a citizen, whose runaway son had been restored to him, promised to donate a statue depicting the boy looking as perplexed as he did when he was found. Legend also has it that after the theft of the statue by Louis XV's soldiers, the king honoured the Manneken-Pis with the title of Knight of St Louis and donated the costume of a marquis as an apology. This became the first piece in the collection of the Manneken-Pis wardrobe now found in the City Museum in the King's House *(see page 22)*.

Bronze rubbing
As you exit the Grand' Place by the arch that leads into Rue Charles Buls, be sure to pay your respects at the recumbent sculpture of the executed folk hero Everard 't Serclaes *(see below)* – rubbing the smoothly polished bronze is said to impart good luck.

14th-century Brusssels hero Everard 't Serclaes

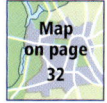

Map on page 32

Miss Pis
At the corner of Impasse de la Fidélité (a street which comes to a dead end at Rue des Bouchers) is Manneken's female counterpart, Jeanneke Pis. This bronze statue, 60cm (23 inches) tall, was created by the sculptor Lucie Genard in 1985.

According to established rules of protocol, the figure wears different uniforms to commemorate different events. For example, on 6 April he wears a uniform of the American military police in honour of the day when the USA entered World War I. On 30 April his garb is the uniform of a French Legionnaire in memory of the French Foreign Legion, and on 3 September the uniform of a guardsman from the Welsh Guards Regiment in celebration of the liberation of Brussels by this regiment in 1944. On 4 September Manneken-Pis wears the uniform of a soldier of the Piron Brigade. This is the anniversary of the day in 1914 when this brigade marched into Brussels. On 15 September he dons the uniform of an RAF pilot in memory of the Battle of Britain and on 27 October the uniform of a US sailor to celebrate Navy Day in America. On 20 November, when students at the University of Brussels honour their patron saint, Manneken-Pis is dressed accordingly.

CHURCH OF OUR LADY

The **Villers Tower** (Tour de Villers) ⑫, located on Rue de Villers, is a remnant of the former city wall dating from the 12th century.

One of the loveliest churches in Brussels is the ★ **Church of Our Lady of the Chapel**

Bargain-hunting at the Place du Jeu de Balle flea market

(L'Eglise Notre-Dame-de-la-Chapelle) **⓭**. Back in the Middle Ages the church was the centre of a working-class neighbourhood, today known as Les Marolles. It became a place of pilgrimage for its relics of the True Cross. The building provides evidence of several centuries of Brabant art and architecture. It was begun in the 12th century, but the nave seen today was mainly constructed in the 15th century, while the steeple dates from the early 18th century. Extensive restoration was carried out during the 19th century. The church is a harmonious union of a variety of architectural styles. A small Romanesque tower in the southern transept dates from the earliest epoch. Elements of early Gothic can also be found, while the steeple with its onion dome is in Renaissance style. Look for the tympanum above the west door, which has a sculpture by Constantin Meunier.

The interior of the church houses a carved wooden pulpit by Pierre Demis Plumier (early 18th-century), a 16th-century confessional, 17th century pillar sculptures and the tombs of Peter Brueghel the Elder and François Anneessens, an 18th-century guildsman, whose execution in 1719 put an abrupt end to a revolt against Austrian rule.

THE OLD CITY WALLS

The tour now leaves the Place de la Chapelle along the Rue Haute behind the church and continues north (in the direction of the city centre), turning right at **Anneessens Tower** (La Tour d'Anneessens) **⓮** into Rue de Rollebeek. This two-storey, circular fortified tower, also called Tour d'Angle, is another remnant of the old city wall dating from the 12th century, and was only rediscovered in 1957.

THE GRAND SABLON

A centre for antique trading, and one of the city's most attractive squares is **★★ Grand-Sablon Square** (Place du Grand-Sablon) **⓯**, which was, in the 12th century, a road laid with sand (*sable*), hence the name. Today, it's a good place to sit

Star Attraction
• Grand Sablon Square

Below: Manneken-Pis
Bottom: Marolles' church

Map on page 32

Burial chapel

In the church of Notre-Dame is the burial chapel of the family Thurn and Taxis, who initiated, from Brussels, the international postal service using a horse relay system.

on a terrace with a drink and watch the world go by, or take a break in one of the pâtisseries and tearooms selling delicious cakes and chocolates. A lively antiques, antiquarian book and flea market is held here every weekend; it's fun to browse but bargains are thin on the ground.

THE SABLON'S CHURCH

At the corner of the square and Petite Rue des Minimes is the **Postal Museum** (Musée Postal) which documents the history of the postal system with a complete collection of Belgian as well as foreign stamps. It also houses a number of old and modern telecommunications devices. Between the Grand and Petit Sablon, on Rue de la Régence, is the ★★ **Church of Our Lady of the Victories** (Notre-Dame-des-Victoires-au-Sablon) ⓰. It dates from the 15th–16th century and is recognised as one of the most superb examples of High-Gothic architecture in Belgium. The church, completely restored at the end of the 19th century, owes its magnificence to the archers guild of Brussels, which was instrumental in its construction. Noteworthy in the interior: a gilt wooden chandelier, a candelabra dating from 1631, a carved wooden pulpit from 1697 and the murals in the choir. The Sablon is particularly inviting in the evening, when the stained-glass windows of the church are illuminated.

Rue de la Régence serves here as a link between Routes 2 and 3 (Museum of Historical Art, *see page 26*).

Statue of craftsman in the Petit-Sablon Square

PEACEFUL PARK

Route 3 continues from the church across Rue de la Régence to the small park created in 1890 at **Petit-Sablon Square** (Place du Petit-Sablon) ⓱. This was formerly a cemetery and is surrounded by an interesting wrought-iron fence. Small bronze statues, 48 in number, each represent the craftsmen's guilds of the 16th century. The art nouveau railings were designed by Paul Hankar. In the middle of the gardens is a bronze group depicting the Counts of Egmont and Hoorn, martyrs of the resistance movement, beheaded by the merciless Duke of Alba in 1568 for their part in an uprising, surrounded by renowned Humanists such as Mercator, Van Orley, Dodennée and others. It's a pleasant place to stop for a rest. The Brussels Conservatory is at the corner of Rue de la Régence and the square (house No 17), in a building constructed by Cluysenaar in 1876–7. Behind Petit-Sablon Square, on Rue aux Laines, stands the **Egmont Palace** (Palais d'Egmont) **18**. Originally constructed in the 16th century, it was acquired by the Arenberg family in the 18th century and renovated in Classical style. Today the palace is the residence of the Belgian Foreign Minister and is not open to the public. Its historic significance – Louis XV, Christine of Sweden and Voltaire resided here – was enhanced in 1972 when the Treaty of Accession to the European Community was signed here by the United Kingdom, Ireland and Denmark.

PALACE OF JUSTICE

Adjacent to the palace is a lovely park, parallel to Rue aux Laines (no access from this side). This leads to Poelaert Square and thus to one of the most conspicuous buildings in Brussels, the ★ **Palace of Justice** (Palais de Justice) **19**. Construction was

Star Attraction
• **Church of our Lady of the Victories**

Below: relax in the Petit-Sablon Square
Bottom: detail on the monumental Palace of Justice

Map on page 32

Pointed message

It was surely no coincidence that the colossal Palais de Justice was built on a hill dominating — you might almost say frowning balefully down upon — the city's rebelliously inclined, working-class Marolles district.

begun in 1866 by the architect Joseph Poelaert (1817–79) but was not completed until 1883, after his death. The dome towers 104m (333ft) above the city, making it visible far and wide.

With an area of 25,000sq m (30,000sq yards), 27 assembly rooms and 245 smaller chambers, it is a monumental construction, probably the largest ever built in the 19th century. Created in Graeco-Roman style, the building was erected on the site of the Brussels gallows. Its powerful form was designed to be reminiscent of the architecture of late antiquity as well as Egypt and Asia Minor. On both sides of the huge outdoor steps are colossal statues of Demosthenes, Lycurgus, Cicero and Ulpianus. Inside, the staircase of the entrance hall and the great hall crowned by the dome are architecturally of the greatest significance. The Palace of Justice still functions as the supreme court of law for Belgium.

THE MAROLLES

Route 3 is probably the longest of the downtown walking tours described in this book. Those who wish to return to the starting point from here can walk around the Palace of Justice and follow Rue de Wynants and Rue du Faucon to Rue Haute, thus returning to the Grand' Place.

It is also possible to cross from Poelaert Square

Church of our Lady of the Victories on Grand-Sablon Square

to the Place Louise metro station, taking Line 2 to Arts-Loi and changing there to Line 1 which leads to the Central Station near the Town Hall.

Those who wish to continue on this walk, however, can follow Route 3 to the southern tip of the city centre. From the Palace of Justice, walk along Rue aux Laines to the end. Here, a short side street leads to a park between Boulevard de Waterloo and Avenue de la Porte de Hal. This is the only tower still standing from the second medieval city wall; it dates from the year 1381 and was restored in 1868–70, the gate called the **Porte de Hal ⓴** (open Tues–Sun 10am–5pm; admission fee).

From here, Rue Haute, the main drag running through the interesting Marolles quarter, leads north and back into the city centre. On the right-hand side of the street, in the complex of the St Pierre Hospital (entrance at Rue Haute 298a) is the **Museum of Public Welfare** (Musée de l'Assistance Publique; open Wed only 2–4pm) ㉑. Paintings, sculptures and tapestries, goldsmiths' crafts and antique furniture bequeathed by the most important charitable organisations of earlier ages, present a characteristic picture of the artistic milieu of Brussels and Brabant in the 15th to 18th century.

Rue Haute and the parallel Rue Blaes lead again past the Church of Our Lady of the Chapel and the Anneessens Tower (Tour d'Angle, *see page 35*) seen earlier on this tour. From here, one of two routes is possible. On the other side of the Boulevard de l'Empereur, either cross Place Dinant, passing the Manneken-Pis again (the monument is quite small and easily missed) or continue more or less in a straight line along Rue de l'Escalier, Place de la Vieille Halle-aux-Blés, Place Saint-Jean and Rue de la Violette to the Grand' Place. Although there are no sights of note along these streets, it is a charming, if slightly delapidated, part of town that provides an interesting peek behind the scenes of the Old Town. An excellent Sunday morning flea market is held on **Place du Jeu de Balle**. Pieter Breughel lived at 132 Rue Haute, and the nearby square named after him is lined with stylish restaurants.

Below: entrance hall of the Palace of Justice
Bottom: a stroll in the Marolles

Map
on page
41

Vanished stream
Place St-Géry used to be an island in the River Senne, until the river was pushed underground. The Brussels City Museum *(see page 23)* contains fascinating paintings depicting this area when a river flowed through it.

4: St Catherine's Square

Notre-Dame-du-Bon-Secours – Notre-Dame-aux-Riches-Claires – Place St-Géry – St Catherine's Square – Black Tower – De Brouckère Square – Boulevard Anspach – Stock Exchange – Falstaff – St Nicholas Church

This route also leaves the Grand' Place via Rue Charles Buls and its extension, Rue de l'Etuve. At the Manneken-Pis *(see page 33)*, however, it turns right into Rue des Grands Carmes. At the end of this street, after the intersection with the main street Rue du Midi, is the ★**Church of Notre-Dame-du-Bon-Secours** ㉒. It is built in the Flemish Renaissance style of the 17th century and contains a statue of the Holy Virgin which is reputed to have miraculous powers.

The church is at the corner of Rue du Marché-au-Charbon and Rue du Jardin des Olives. The latter street ends at the Boulevard Anspach. Follow this boulevard north to the Stock Exchange (Bourse; *see page 43*). To see other sights in the western part of the city centre, however, cross the main street and take the next left.

BIRTHPLACE OF THE CITY

Interior of Notre-Dame-du-Bon-Secours

Rue des Riches-Claires leads to the church of **Notre-Dame-aux-Riches-Claires** ㉓ (open for

Mass only). Its gables depict a typical Brussels conception of Italian Renaissance. It is the work of Luc Fayd'herbe (1617–97), a pupil of Rubens known above all for his creation of colossal statues adorning the pillars of the church nave. Taking Rue de la Grande Ile leads you to **Place St-Géry**, the very birthplace of the city: it is the site of a castle occupied by Charles Duke of Lorraine in 979, the year celebrated as the founding of Brussels. These days, the square is lined with cafés and is buzzing until dawn every weekend.

Star Attraction
• **St Catherine's Square**

THE FISH MARKET

Nearby Rue Antoine Dansaert, with its designer shops and trendy bars and restaurants, leads to ★★ **St Catherine's Square** (Place Ste-Catherine) **24**. This is the city's old port – central Brussels was linked with Antwerp and the North Sea by a canal until 1853, when railways and the threat of flooding rendered it obsolete. The square then became a fish market, which explains the many excellent fish restaurants surrounding it. St Catherine's Church, originally dating from the 14th–15th century, was reconstructed in a mixture of Romanesque and Renaissance style in 1854–5 by Joseph Poelaert, the architect of the Palace of Justice. The 17th-century St Catherine's Tower (Tour Ste-Catherine) is the only remaining part of this church's predecessor. In the left-hand aisle stands the Black Madonna, dating from the 14th–15th century. The statue was originally carved from light-coloured stone, but over the years it has become almost completely blackened.

The **Black Tower** (Tour Noire) is one of the rare remains of the first city wall from the 12th century. Crossing over Samedi Square and following along Rue du Cyprès, the route leads to the **Beguine Church** (St-Jean-Baptiste-au-Béguinage) **25**. Originally the church was a Gothic basilica. It was renovated in 1657–76, at which time the present-day facade, a

The Black Tower on St Catherine's Square

Map on page 41

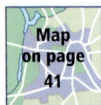

Water feature
The fountain in the pool near the church on St Catherine's Square depicts St Michael slaying the devil and originally stood on nearby De Brouckère Square. It was erected in honour of Jules Anspach, mayor of Brussels 1863–79 and prime mover behind the construction of the city's grand avenues.

splendid example of the Flemish exuberance of Belgian baroque, was created. The Beguine community itself, which totalled 1,200 members in its heyday, was dissolved in the 19th century.

CINEMAS AND SHOPS

We now head along Rue de Laeken and Rue des Hirondelles directly to the centre of the business and entertainment area of Brussels, **De Brouckère Square** (Place de Brouckère) ㉖. It is here that Boulevard Anspach leading from the south and Boulevard Adolphe-Max from the north, merge. Boulevard Anspach is named after the mayor who, after Belgium's independence in 1830, ordered the obliteration of the River Senne and in its place the construction of long wide boulevards in a style befitting a modern nation state. With its neon-lit cinemas and bars, this is a busy area at night, although some of the narrow streets and nightclubs off the main drag are decidedly seedy.

By now this route has probably turned into a shopping spree along the busy Boulevard Anspach which leads south from De Brouckère Square past the Centre Monnaie with its large, modern shopping arcade. A perfect place to stop for a restoring drink is the lovely **Hôtel Métropole**, with its terrace café and elegant, comfortable lounge bar.

The Stock Exchange (La Bourse)

Before returning to the Grand' Place, the route leads to Place de la Bourse, a square located directly on Boulevard Anspach, and the site of the **Stock Exchange** (La Bourse) ❷❼, the centre of Brussels' financial life. It was constructed in 1868–75 in neo-baroque style; a relief on the facade depicts Belgium's defence through commerce and industry. Passing through a glass door leading to an antechamber, you can observe the stockbrokers' activity. Underneath the adjacent Rue de la Bourse, remains of 13th-century Brussels were unearthed by archaelogists some years ago. Their discoveries form the **Bruxella 1238 Museum** and offer a fascinating glimpse of the early development of the city.

THE FALSTAFF

Next door on Rue Henri Maus is the famous ★★ **Falstaff** bar . It is a glorious example of Belgian art nouveau and was once the haunt of intellectuals and artists. Nowadays it is popular with locals and tourists alike, and stays open till well past midnight for drinks and snacks.

Diagonally across from the Falstaff is the **Church of St Nicholas** (L'Eglise Saint-Nicolas) ❷❽, dedicated to the patron saint of merchants. As one of Brussels' oldest churches, its historical development mirrors that of the city. It has been repeatedly renovated over the centuries and in 1955 received a totally new facade. The interior of the church is richly decorated with works of art: the altar in the left aisle is adorned with a 15th-century Madonna; the pillar on the right-hand side of the choir supports a Spanish figure of Christ dating from the 16th century; the painting of the Virgin and Child Asleep is attributed to Rubens.

A copper shrine in front of the pulpit recalls the Martyrs of Gorcum, who were put to death in Brielle (near Rotterdam) after suffering unspeakable torture at the hands of the Protestant Dutch privateers known as the 'Sea Beggars'.

From here, along Rue au Beurre, it is only a short way back to the Town Hall on the Grand' Place.

Star Attraction
• **The Falstaff**

Below: dish of the day
Bottom: church of St Nicholas

5: Around Rue Neuve

Finistère Church – Rue Neuve – North Station – Botanical Garden – Martyrs' Square – Théâtre Royal de la Monnaie

Map on page 45

Ring route

The boulevard ring was constructed along the lines of the old city wall which until that time had encircled the Old Town. The road, with a length of 7km (4 miles), was built in the middle of the 19th century. It has been modernised since then and is now free of crossings, running through tunnels and over bridges. The ring is the major motor route within the city; without it Brussels, with the volume of traffic passing through it today, would be even more chaotic.

This route, leading through the northern sector of the city centre, leaves the Grand' Place to the left of the King's House via the tiny Rue Chair et Pain (Meat and Bread Street). Shortly thereafter it turns left into Rue du Marché-aux-Herbes. This, and the adjoining Rue du Marché-aux-Poulets, lead directly to Boulevard Anspach. It is also possible to take the first street to the right, Rue de la Fourche, walking through the arcades of **Galerie du Centre** ㉙ and Galerie St-Honoré, with their eclectic range of slightly off-beat shops; also, in the former gallery, you'll find Au bon Vieux Temps, a traditional brown bar and ideal stopping-off point for a glass of ale or wine. Nearby Rue du Marché-aux-Poulets leads to Boulevard Anspach and Place de Brouckère ㉚, which are described in Route 4 *(see page 42)*, where this route turns right, towards the north.

Finistère Church on Rue Neuve

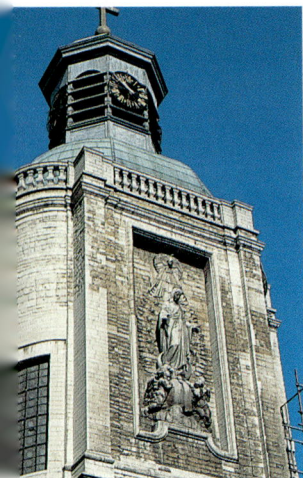

RUE NEUVE

Along Boulevard Adolphe-Max, a wide shopping avenue heading north from De Brouckère Square, is, at the corner of a tiny street of the same name, the **Finistère church** (L'Eglise au Finistère) ㉛. It was built in 1708 and contains a Gothic statue of Mary which comes from Aberdeen, called Notre-Dame-du-Bon-Succès. The entrance is on the pedestrianised **Rue Neuve**. This is one of the city's main shopping streets, with all the major international fashion chains and the large City 2 mall covering four floors.

Follow Boulevard Adolphe-Max or Rue Neuve further north to Place Rogier ㉜, a major traffic junction. This is the intersection of the north–south boulevard, which links the North Station (Gare du Nord) with the South Station (Gare du Midi), and the congested boulevard ring, a 4-lane highway which surrounds the city centre *(see box, left)*.

RAILWAY MUSEUM

About 500m north of Charles Rogier Square on
Rue du Progrès, skirting the old red-light area,
is the North Station and the ★ **Railway Museum**
(Musée du Chemin de Fer) ❸❸ (open Mon–Fri and
1st Sat of month 9am–4.30pm; free). Of great
interest to railway buffs, it contains models, loco-

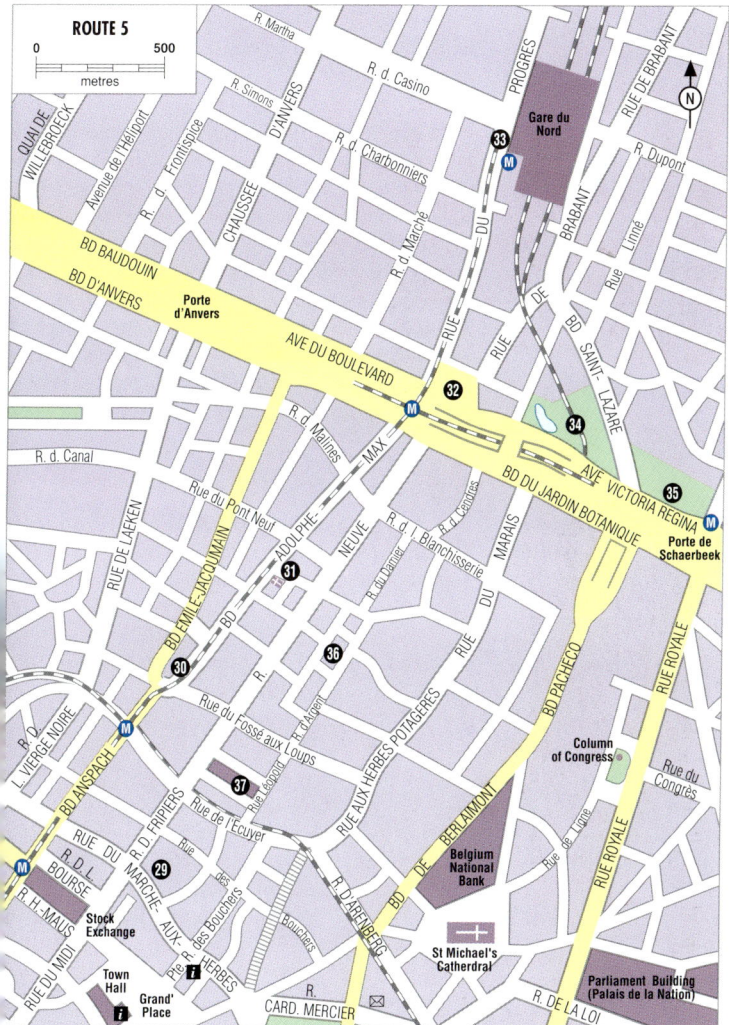

ROUTE 5

0   500
metres

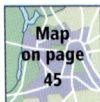

Map on page 45

Royal Mint
The Théâtre Royal de la Monnaie occupies the site of the former royal mint, which minted coins for the Duchy of Brabant.

motives, uniforms and other material depicting the development of the Belgian railway system. The entrance is at Rue du Progrès 76.

Also on the other side of the ring, bearing the appropriate name Boulevard du Jardin Botanique, is the **Botanical Garden** (Jardin Botanique) ❸❹. As a shortcut from the Finistère Church, you can cross to Rue aux Choux, then take Rue du Marais to the ring. These public gardens extend eastward from the original site and form one of Belgium's most important collections of exotic trees and plants. The original gardens were laid out here in 1826–30, when this area was a quiet and leafy backwater outside the main town. The **grand greenhouse** ❸❺ at the corner of Rue Royale and Rue Botanique was built in 1826. It is constructed of iron and glass with rows of ionic pillars. Because further expansion on this site was not possible, a new botanical garden was created in 1944 at the Domein Bouchout in the village of Meise *(see page 55)* and the green house is now the cultural centre of the French-speaking community and holds concerts in the summer.

MARTYRS' SQUARE

Restaurants on the Petite Rue des Bouchers do their best to attract tourists

The return route leads parallel to Boulevard Adolphe-Max, along Rue des Cendres, Rue du Damier and Rue des Oeillets, and on to **Martyrs'**

Square (Place des Martyrs) **㊱**. The architect Claude Antoine Fisco designed this square in an austere neoclassical style. Unfortunately, many of its buildings were later abandoned and left to decay, but renovation has been underway and many of the buildings are now in use again. The 450 heroes who gave their lives fighting the Dutch in the 1830 revolution are buried beneath the monument, Belgia, which stands in the centre of the square.

THEATRE ROYAL

The **Théâtre Royal de la Monnaie ㊲** has a reputation as one of the finest opera houses in the world. In 1855, a fire destroyed extensive sections of the building; restoration was completed by Joseph Poleaert (architect of the Palace of Justice) and the auditorium was greatly extended. Today, the theatre hosts a full and varied program of opera and classical concerts (box office open Tues–Sat 11am–6pm, tel: 070-233939).

The Monnaie theatre holds a special place in Belgium's history. In 1830, the opera *Masianello* (also known as *La Muette de Portici*), by Daniel François Esprit Auber and based on the Neapolitan Revolution of 1647, had been scheduled for performance at the opera house, but, following unrest in the city, the authorities had felt it wise to postpone its run. The première was finally held on 25 August before a packed house. Its effect on the audience was electrifying. As the opera progressed they became increasingly agitated, and when, in Act IV, the call to arms rang out, it could not be contained. With patriotic cries on their lips they streamed out of the auditorium towards the houses occupied by Dutch families, and then to the municipal park. The revolution had begun, and independence soon followed.

Head back to the Grand' Place via Rue de l'Ecuyer, Rue des Dominicains and **Petite Rue de Bouchers** in the **Îlot Sacré**, where you'll find scores of restaurants, two of the most reliable being Chez Léon and Aux Armes de Bruxelles. Alternatively, continue along Rue de l'Ecuyer and return via the Galeries Saint-Hubert.

Below: Théâtre Royal de la Monnaie
Bottom: the Botanical Garden

Map on page 49

Royal facade
The elegant classical facade of the Galeries Royales Saint-Hubert is decorated with columns and a central motif that proclaims *Omnibus omnia* – everything for everyone.

Below: Stained-glass window, St Michael's Cathedral
Bottom: the Galeries Royales St Hubert

6: Galeries Royales & Cathedral

Galeries Royales Saint-Hubert – St Michael's Cathedral – Column of Congress – Parliament Building – Brussels Park – Royal Palace

The last route through the city centre leaves the Grand' Place via Rue de la Colline, the same path as Route 2 *(see page 25)*, and leads to the eastern part of the downtown area. The two routes join at the southern end of Brussels Park, in front of the Royal Palace *(see page 31)* thus making it possible to combine both routes into one longer tour.

At the end of Rue de la Colline, across Rue du Marché-aux-Herbes, are the elegant ★★ **Galeries Royales Saint-Hubert** ❸, built in 1846 as the first glass-covered shopping arcade in Europe. The main gallery has a length of 200m (650ft). Rue des Bouchers cuts through the middle, dividing the arcade into the Galerie de la Reine (Queen's Gallery) and the Galerie du Roi (King's Gallery). A third section, branching off to the left from the latter is the Galerie des Princes (Gallery of Princes). This extends to Rue des Dominicains. The Galeries are a good place to buy high-class chocolates and genuine Brussels lace.

SUDDEN DEATH

At the end of the main gallery and across to the right, on Rue Montagne des Herbes Potagères, is the much loved Brussels tavern, the ★**Mort Subite** ❹, once the haunt of singer Jacques Brel, a fine place to rest your feet and sample some local ale. The route now turns into Rue d'Arenberg which leads to Boulevard de l'Impératrice. To the right, on this boulevard, is the Central Station of Brussels (Gare Centrale) ❹, first opened in 1952. To the left is the huge Belgian National Bank complex ❹ which was built in 1860.

ST MICHAEL'S CATHEDRAL

The next sight is the powerful Gothic structure of Brussels' principal place of worship. Its complete name is the Church of St Michael and St Gudula

(Collégiale Saint-Michel et Sainte-Gudule), but it is more usually referred to simply as ★★ **St Michael's Cathedral** (Cathédrale Saint-Michel) **42**. The nave and aisles, after renovations carried out over several years, have been restored to their original beauty. The impressive structure was built in 1226 when it became apparent that the existing Romanesque church was too small. The main elements of its facade are vertical, making it more reminiscent of German Gothic than of the French architecture of this period. The choir, transept and southern aisle date from the 13th century while the northern aisle, nave and both of the unfinished 69-m (226-ft) high towers are from the 14th–15th century. The side chapel, housing the

Star Attraction
• **St Michael's Cathedral**

ROUTE 6

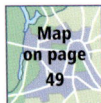

Map on page 49

Pure beauty
Victor Hugo considered the magnificent St Michael's Cathedral to be the "purest flowering of the Gothic style".

tombs of the Dukes of Brabant, was added between the 16th and 17th centuries.

The stained-glass windows in the choir, the transept and some of the chapels are especially beautiful. Many of these magnificent windows were created from drawings by Van Orley and were a gift from Charles V and his family. The carved pulpit from 1699 and the Brussels tapestries woven by Van der Borght in 1785 (displayed only on religious holidays) are of particular note.

The church was restored in the 19th century, at which time the huge outdoor steps were added. Other sights in the interior of the church include:

In the nave: statues of the apostles on the pillars, carved by Jérôme Duquesnoy the Younger (Paul, Matthew, Bartholomew, Thomas), by Luc Fayd'herbe (Simon), by Jan van Milder (Philip, Andrew) and by Tobias de Lelis (Peter, John); the pulpit by Henri F Verbruggen (1699) depicting the banishment from Paradise; the animals, at the steps, by Van der Haeghen (1780); and the 16th-century stained-glass window of the portal portraying The Last Judgment by J de Vriendt.

In the transept: stained-glass windows by Barend van Orley depicting Charles V, Isabella of Portugal and Louis the Great of Hungary with his wife Maria as well as paintings by Michael Coxie *(Crucifixion and Entombment, The Life of St Gudula).*

Facade of St Michael's Cathedral

In the choir: late 16th-century stained-glass above the high altar, depicting from left to right Maximilian of Austria and Mary of Burgundy, Philip the Fair and Joanna of Castile, Charles V and his brother Ferdinand, Philip II and Mary of Portugal, Philibert of Savoy and Margaret of Austria. Behind the high altar is the tomb of Duke John II of Brabant, who died in 1312, and his wife. Across from this is the tomb of Archduke Ernst (died 1595) with the statue by Robert de Nole.

In the Chapel of the Virgin (Chapelle de la Vierge): stained-glass windows by Jean de la Baer (1656–63) based on drawings by van Thulden as well as portraits of the donor Emperor Ferdinand III and his wife Eleonore, Emperor Leopold I, Archduke Albrecht and Isabella, Archduke Leopold Wilhelm.

In the Chapel of the Miracle of the Holy Sacrament (Chapelle du Saint-Sacrement de Miracle): stained-glass windows depicting the miracle of the sacrament. According to biblical legend, the stolen Host began to flower, thus leading to the discovery of the culprit, who was burned alive as punishment. In the lower part of the window are portraits of the donors Catherine and John III of Portugal, Louis of Hungary and Maria, King Francis I of France and Eleonore as well as Ferdinand I and Anna of Poland. The stained-glass windows were designed by Coxie and Van Orley.

Below: impressive interior of St Michael's Cathedral
Bottom: the Column of Congress celebrates Belgian independence

COLUMN OF CONGRESS

Behind the church and the National Bank, beginning at the corner of Rue de la Banque and Rue des Bois-Sauvage, is Rue de Ligne which leads to the 47-m (154-ft) high **Column of Congress** (Colonne du Congrès) ❸ in Congress Square. Built in 1850–9 and designed by Joseph Poelaert, it commemorates the National Congress which created the Belgian constitution after independence in 1830. At the base of the column, a flame burns over the Grave of the Unknown Soldier, a memorial to the victims of both world wars. Behind the monument, an esplanade offers a good view over the city skyline.

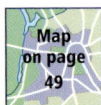

Map on page 49

I-Spy
At the Parliament, visitors can watch a video tape tour of the building or can observe a parliamentary session from the gallery.

THE BELGIAN PARLIAMENT

From this northernmost point of the walking tour, the path leads south along Rue Royale, continuing to the corner of Rue de la Loi where the **Parliament Building** (Palais de la Nation) ④④ is located. Both houses of the Belgian parliament, the House of Representatives and the Senate, convene here. The offices of various ministries are housed in the part of the palace adjacent to the parliament sector.

In former times, the complex was the seat of the Advisory Council of the Duchy of Brabant. The structure was originally built from 1779–83 by Guimard. It was rebuilt about 100 years later (1884–7) after having been destroyed by fire. From here, Rue de la Loi leads east across the boulevard ring to the European Union headquarters at Rond-Point Schuman. A little further on is Cinquantenaire Park and Palace with a number of important museums. These sights are described in Route 8 *(see page 58)*.

Below: relaxing in Brussels Park
Bottom: the Parliament Building

BRUSSELS PARK

The classical facade of the Palais de la Nation looks out over a square of the same name. Beyond the square is ★**Brussels Park** (Parc de Bruxelles) ④⑤, the hunting grounds of the dukes of Brabant in medieval times. It was converted in 1776 to French gardens by the Austrian Anton Zinner. This is a popular place to take a stroll and at 13ha (32 acres) in size, it is the largest park in the city centre and a model of geometrical precision. Its paths are lined with trees and numerous statues. Within the park is the Royal Park Theatre (Théâtre Royal du Parc), located in the northeast corner.

At the southern end of the park is the **Royal Palace** ④⑥ while the Italian Renaissance-style **Palace of the Academies** ④⑦ is located along the southeastern side. Both of these buildings are described in Route 2 *(see page 31)*. To return to the starting point from here, follow Route 2 in either direction, returning directly to the Grand' Place or passing via Place Royale and Mont des Arts.

7: Brussels Harbour & Heysel

Brussels Harbour – Laeken – Royal Palace – Domein Bouchout (Botanical Garden) – Grimbergen Abbey – Centenaire Halls – Atomium

This route is best done by car, although many of the sights can be reached by public transport from the centre of Brussels. Almost all of the main streets exiting the northern part of the boulevard ring between Place Sainctelette in the northwest and Porte de Schaerbeek in the northeast lead to the park-like northern sector of Brussels. These streets all feed into Avenue de la Reine which crosses the Sea Canal immediately north of **Brussels Harbour ❹❽** and leads to the large park grounds of Laeken. First, however, a few words about the harbour, located between Avenue du Port and Allée Verte.

The Chinese Pavilion was built in Shanghai and assembled in Belgium

BRUSSELS PORT AND CANAL

As early as 1434, as the Senne became increasingly silted, Brussels was given permission by Duke Philip the Good to dredge a channel in the river. But this measure proved unsatisfactory and in 1477 Mary of Burgundy granted permission to dig a canal alongside the river, designed to link the Senne to the Rupel at Willebroek. It was completed in 1561 and shortly thereafter three harbour

Map
below

ROUTE 7

0   2

kilometres

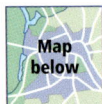

basins were constructed in Brussels. The canal was first deepened in 1819–36. Two phases of expansion, beginning in 1902, eventually converted the Willebroek into a sea canal. A sea harbour, with all of the necessary technical facilities, was also constructed at that time. In 1922 the canal was finally opened to ocean-going vessels with a draught of up to 5.8m (19ft). The Brussels port was then linked to the southern Belgian industrial region via the Charleroi Canal and, via the Willebroek Canal, to the Scheldt and thus right to the open sea.

On the other side of the canal, Avenue de la Reine leads into Avenue du Parc Royal. Here, on the left, is the **Church of Notre-Dame-de-Laeken ④**, about 4km (2.5 miles) from the Grand' Place. It was constructed from 1854–72 by Poelaert in memory of Louise-Maria, the first queen of Belgium. A miraculous Virgin, dating from the 13th century, attracts many worshippers. Aside from the royal crypt, this church also contains the tombs of many prominent Belgian personalities.

ROYAL GREENHOUSES

Park Avenue continues north from the church through several curves. The royal domain of Laeken (Domaine Royal) is on the right. This is the location of the huge **Royal Palace** (Château Royal) **⑤**. The palace, still the residence of the royal family, is closed to the public. It was built by Montoyer in the second half of the 18th century and later renovated under Leopold II in Louis XVI style. It was expanded by Girault in 1903. The main attraction is the series of 11 beautiful ★★**Royal Greenhouses** (Serres Royales) **⑤** connected by glass passageways, built in Leopold II's reign between 1876–95.

The most magnificent part of this exotic world of plants is the winter garden. The

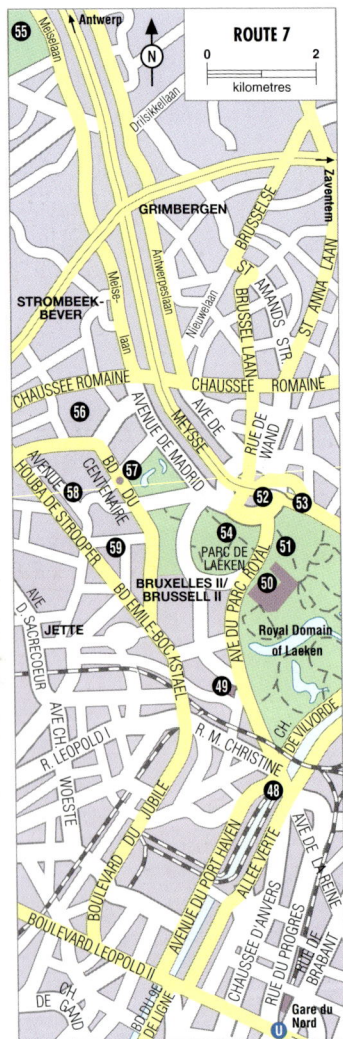

greenhouses are only open to the public for two weeks in April and May, and are well worth visiting if you can. The opening times are announced in the newspapers and on the radio.

ORIENTAL FOLLIES

Just a short distance from the greenhouses is the **Neptune Fountain** (Fontaine de Neptunel) ❷, a replica of the fountain created by sculptor Jean de Bologne in 1566 for Piazza del Nuttuno in Bologna. Nearby, skirted by the busy motorway linking Brussels with Antwerp, is the ★**Chinese Pavilion** (Pavillon Chinois) ❸ (open Tues–Sun 10am–4.45pm; admission fee). In 1901, Leopold II commissioned the Paris architect Alexandre Marcel to have it built in Shanghai and assembled in Brussels. Today it houses a priceless collection of Chinese porcelain. The nearby ★**Japanese Tower** (open Tues–Sun 10am– 4.45pm; admission fee), with its ornate interior, is another example of Leopold's taste for oriental artefacts, which were very much in vogue at the time.

Across from the Royal Palace, on the west side of Park Avenue, is the Laeken Public Park (Parc de Laeken), site of the **Belvédère Palace** ❹, which was built for Viscount de Walckiers in 1788 and is today the residence of the Prince of Liège. In the middle of the central traffic circle (Place de la Dynastie) is a monument to Leopold, first king of the Belgians.

> **Bonaparte's place**
> In 1804, Napoleon Bonaparte rescued the Royal Palace from total ruin and used it as his residence until his defeat at Waterloo in 1815. It was here, in 1812, that Napolean signed the declaration of war against Russia.

Giant waterlilies at the National Botanical Garden of Belgium

NATIONAL BOTANICAL GARDEN

At this point a decision must be made, whether to take a detour to the ★★ **National Botanical Garden of Belgium** ❺ (open daily 9.30am–5pm) at the Domein van Bouchout *(see also Map, page 74).* If you choose to visit the garden, drive onto the Antwerp motorway at the northern end of Park Avenue and take the exit for Strombeek-Bever. The next exit, Meise, is beyond Bouchout. The domain is located at the southern end of the town of Meise. The Botanical Garden extends to 93ha (230 acres) and was moved here in 1944 when the

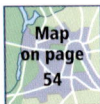

Map
on page
54

Moat House
The moated castle in the centre of the Botanical Garden served as the occasional residence of Empress Charlotte, widow of the executed Emperor of Mexico and the sister of Leopold II. The castle's tower dates from the 14th century.

collection outgrew its former location on the ring near the North Station. These peaceful and beautiful gardens contain a huge collection of flowers, shrubs and trees from all over the world. The huge greenhouse, named the Plant Palace, contains rainforest plants from Asia, Africa and South America, as well as giant waterlilies.

Grimbergen Abbey, only 7km (4 miles) from Meise, is situated directly on the road between Meise and Vilvoorde. Noteworthy in its unique baroque church of St Servais are the confessional, pulpit and choir pews as well as a ceiling fresco in the vestry. The abbey is the origin of the excellent Grimbergen beer, which was brewed here for centuries, but is now produced by Maes elsewhere in Belgium. However, you can still sample a glass in the abbey's café.

HEYSEL AND THE ATOMIUM

In the Heysel section of town is the International Conference Centre (Centre International de Conférences) with the **Centenaire Halls** (Palais du Centenaire) ❺❻. These halls, which also serve as the site of the Brussels International Sample Trade Fair, were originally built in 1935 and then expanded for the World Exhibition of 1958. The name derives from the centennial of Belgian independence. The complex of buildings is one of the largest exhibition and trade fair centres in Europe. At the end of Boulevard du Centenaire, which leads from the exhibition halls back towards the city, is the ★ **Atomium** ❺❼ (closed for renovations until January 2006). This bizarre-looking structure was designed for the 1958 World Exhibition, to symbolise the potential of Belgian industry in the optimisim of the post-war period. After the exhibition, the City of Brussels placed a formal request to keep its new landmark. With a height of 102m (335ft), it is based on the structure of an iron molecule, enlarged to 165 billion times its original size. The nine atoms are depicted by nine hollow steel spheres, each with a diameter of 18m (59ft). There were nine Belgian provinces in 1958 which each sphere represents. After dark, the nine

St Servais in Grimbergen Abbey is a typical example of Belgian baroque

spheres are illuminated by alternating, revolving lights. An express lift in the central connecting strut takes you to the highest of the nine spheres. The numerous windows provide a breathtaking panorama of the city. After dark, points of light skip from one sphere to the next, symbolising the path of the electrons around the atomic nucleus. It has to be said that the Atomium is most impressive when viewed from a distance.

The **Brussels Planetarium** ❺❽ (open Mon–Fri 9am–4.30pm, 1st and 3rd Sun of month and every Sun in summer 1.30–4pm; admission fee) is located on Avenue de Bouchout which leads westwards from the Atomium. The Heysel sports stadium ❺❾ is also located on this street.

BRUPARCK

A treat for the kids near the Atomium is the gigantic amusement park, ★★ **Bruparck**. As well as bars, restaurants and a carousel, Mini-Europe (open daily late Mar–June and Sept 9.30am–5pm; July–Aug 9.30am–7pm, mid-July–mid-Aug Fri–Sun closes 11pm; Oct–Dec and 1st week Jan 10am–5pm; admission fee) containing miniature replicas of European sights, the aquatic fun-park Océade and Kinopolis, the cinema complex and IMAX theatre, are all extremely popular.

Star Attraction
• **Bruparck**

Below: the Atomium
Bottom: Bruparck is popular with both adults and kids.

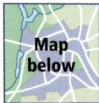

8: European Quarter & Tervuren

East and southeast of the city centre: Route 8a: European quarter – Cinquantenaire Park – Cinquantenaire Arch – Army Museum – Museum of Art and History. Route 8b: Woluwe-St Pierre – Val Duchesse Abbey – Museum of Central Africa in Tervuren

The distance from the centre of the city to the various sights in the east and southeast sections of Brussels varies greatly. The European quarter and Cinquantenaire Park are only about 2km (1.2 miles) from the Parliament Building *(see page 52)* and can be reached by foot along Rue de la Loi, crossing over the eastern section of the ring. Val Duchesse Abbey, on the other hand, is about 7km (4 miles) away and the Museum of Central Africa is 14km (8 miles) from the centre.

Route 8a takes you to the sights which are closer to the centre. If you are travelling by car you can continue to the outskirts of the city, thus reaching Route 8b.

ROUTE 8A: EUROPEAN QUARTER

At the eastern end of Rue de la Loi, surrounding Rond-Point Schuman are the headquarters of the European Union ❻⓿. The main building, the **Berlaymont**, hideous though it may be, is now a well known symbol of the EU, and the bureau-

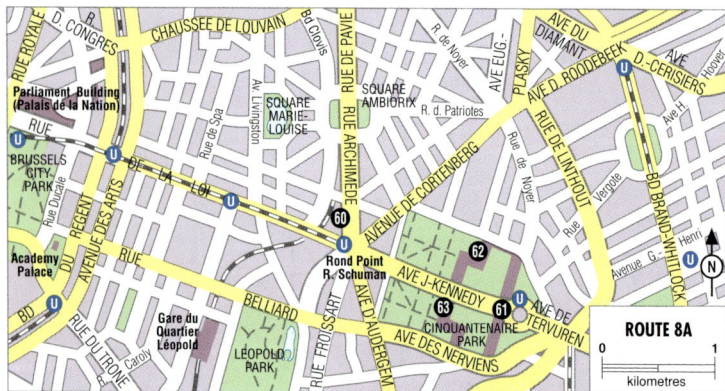

Map below

👁 Art houses

If you're interested in architecture, Rue Archimède leads from Rond-Point Schuman to Square Ambiorix and Square Marie-Louise, which are surrounded by a dazzling array of art nouveau houses. The Tourist Office has information on walks focusing on this subject. If you're hungry, Rue Franklin is a good source of restaurants.

ROUTE 8A

crats took up residence again in November 2004 after years of work to remove the asbestos had been completed. The President of the European Commission and his 24 commissioners (making 25 Commissioners in total, one for each Member State of the EU) also work in the building, while thousands of other Commission officials are scattered throughout the city. The Council of Ministers sits in the massive **Justus Lipsius** building opposite the Berlaymont.

CINQUANTENAIRE PARK

Just east of Rond Point Schuman is ★ **Cinquantenaire Park** (Parc du Cinquantenaire) and the **Cinquantenaire Arch** (Arcade du Cinquantenaire) ❺. The park and palace were built under the reign of Leopold II in honour both of the 50th anniversary of Belgium's independence (hence the French name Cinquantenaire) and of the 1897 World Exhibition held at the eastern edge of the Quartier Léopold. There are several monuments in the park including a Congo memorial and an African memorial, both designed by Thomas Vincotte. A small temple-like structure houses a marble relief entitled *Human Passions* by Jef Lambeaux. On summer evenings the park becomes a drive-in movie theatre, with a vast screen projected across the Arch.

MILITARY MUSEUM

The triumphal arch, visible from afar, is 60m (197ft) wide and 45m (148ft high). It was designed by Girault and links the two wings of the **Cinquantenaire Palace**. The Quadriga over the arch is the work of Vincotte and Lagae. Figures from the Belgian provinces are seen on the column pedestals. The Cinquantenaire Palace, built by Bordiau for the Brussels World Exhibition in 1897, today houses the ★ **Royal Museum of Army and Military History** (Musée Royal de l'Armée et d'Histoire Militaire) ❻ (open Tues–Sun 9am–noon and 1–4.30pm; free) in its north wing. The collections include military relics from

Below: gleaming vintage cars in Autoworld
Bottom: Royal Museums of Art and History

Map on page 58

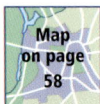

Late for a date

The Cinquantenaire complex was designed to celebrate the 50th anniversary of Belgium's independence in 1880, but most elements missed the celebrations. The triumphal arch wasn't completed until 1888 and the palace until 1897.

the late 18th century onwards, but mainly from World War I, including many exhibits relating to battles which have taken place on Belgian soil. In the section devoted to aircraft are more than 100 historical military planes, including the World War II British classics the Spitfire and the Hurricane. The museum also has a library with 70,000 volumes as well as documents, photos, prints and maps.

CINQUANTENAIRE MUSEUM

In the south wing is the ★★ **Royal Museums of Art and History** (Musées Royaux d'Art et d'Histoire) ❸ (also known as the Cinquantenaire Museum/Musée du Cinquantenaire; open Tues–Fri 9.30am–5pm, Sat–Sun 10am–5pm; admission fee). The collections are divided into the following departments: Ancient Civilisation, European Decorative Arts, Belgian Archaeology and Non-European Civilisation. The impressive exhibits thus provide a grand overview of civilisation over the centuries and are well worth seeing. The museum also has a specialist library which contains classical scientific works and a section specifically for blind people.

The following are a few examples from the wealth of exhibits in the main departments of the museum:

Syrian hunting mosaic dating from the 5th century BC

BELGIAN COLLECTIONS

From prehistoric times: utensils, models of three stages of human development (Neanderthal, Crô-Magnon, Neolithic), models of grottoes in which prehistoric finds were made, the archaeological sites and finds from Bruyère and Baelen, vases, weapons, tombs, tools of polished stone, bronze weapons and tools, archaeological maps of Belgian territory from different eras.

From the Iron Age: weapons, tools, urns and vases, plus early coins.

From the Roman Age in Belgium: the displays comprise finds such as wooden wells, brick and other construction materials, vases, bronzeware, glass and rock crystal objects, tombstones.

From the Frankish Era: weapons, models of living quarters and graves, clasps, jewellery, combs, coins and glassware.

ORIENTAL COLLECTIONS

From Asia Minor: cast of the obelisk of Salmanassar III, various objects of Sumerian and Babylonian origin, cuneiform texts from Babylonia and Assyria dating from the fourth millenium to the second century BC, casts of Assyrian statues and reliefs, a fine collection of pottery cylinders and bricks.

From Upper Egypt (Prehistoric Age): collection of pottery, weapons and stone vases, jewellery, cosmetic objects, an Egyptian tomb whose walls are covered with reliefs and inscriptions.

From Egypt (Old Kingdom): objects from the tombs of the first dynasties, pottery, jewellery, parts of reliefs and statues as well as tombs from the sixth dynasty.

From Egypt (Middle Kingdom and New Kingdom): stone and wood coffins, painted statuettes, vases of clay and stone, jewellery, seals, scarabs, fragments of reliefs from the Temple of Deir el Báhari, bronze items, enamelled pottery as well as wooden and granite statuettes.

From Egypt (New Kingdom): painted pottery vases, part of an obelisk, part of a statue of the

Star Attraction
• **Royal Museums of Art and History**

Below: pottery exhibit from Egypt (Middle Kingdom) Bottom: interior of the museum

Map
on page
58

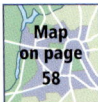

A maze of rooms
There are more than 140 exhibition rooms at the Cinquantenaire Museum, so it makes sense to pick up a free copy of the museum's floor plan from the reception desk before you set out.

wife of King Ramses II, statue of the God Khonsou (21st dynasty), enamelled and faience pottery, amulets, wooden coffins (mostly from Deir el Báhari), parts of a book of the dead and a reconstruction of the tomb of Nakht.

From Egypt (Saitic Era): statuettes from tombs, part of a stone sculpture, mummies and coffins, bronze statuettes of gods and animals, stone vases, pottery and glass, tools and articles of clothing.

From Egypt (Greek-Roman Era): mummies and coffins. Antiquities from Nubia and Sudan.

GREEK AND ROMAN COLLECTIONS

Greek vases from the 5th century BC, vases and vessels from the neolithic and Mycenaean period, vases in geometric style, Etruscan, Ionian and Corinthian vases, red vases with black figures, vessels from Mycenaea (gold, 1500BC), black vases with red figures; 5th- and 6th-century sculptures, sculptures from Greek and Roman times; colossal bronze statue of Septimius Severus, Roman sarcophagus; frescoes from Bosco Reale, lead sarcophagus and bronze works; glasses, combs, jewellery, small bronze trinkets, mirrors; terracotta and Tanagra figures; Phoenician, Hellenistic, Carthaginian and Roman antiquities; casts which illustrate the development of Greek and Roman sculpture.

Fun and games in Cinquantenaire Park

DECORATIVE ARTS

Gothic: Gothic cradle from 1480, 15th-century wood carvings, tapestries from Tournai (15th-century, *Battle of Roncevaux*, *Legend of Hercules*); early 16th-century Brussels tapestries; 15th-century coverlet, Madonna, proclamation from the 15th century (marble, French school of 14th century), tapestry from Tournai (early-16th century, *Sheep Shearing*), tapestries from Brussels (first half of 16th century; *Mary with the Christ Child and St Anne and St Luke*): 15th-century furniture.

Renaissance: Christ on the cross (wood, southern Netherlands, 16th-century); carved and painted wooden portal from the church of St Dymphne in Gheel (1510), remains of a carved altar.

Also numerous interesting exhibitions such as: *Brussels tapestries* from 1513 (the legend of Erkenbald) and from 1518 (legend of Notre-Dame-du-Sablon).

Carvings in the style of Louis XV.

Ivory pieces from the 11th to 14th century and objects created by goldsmiths from the 12th to 18th century.

Enamel pieces from Limoges (13th-century).

Furniture from Louis XV and Louis XVI period.

Clocks and watches from the 17th to 19th century.

Tombstones from the 13th to 17th century.

Porcelain with faiences from Antwerp, Delft and Arnhem; vase from 1562, Chinese porcelain.

Ceramics from Germany, France, England and Belgium; faience pottery from Bernhard Palissy as well as from the Orient.

Cloth and embroidery: silk, embroidered and painted, as well as velvet and vestments.

Belgian lace: this collection is one of the most lovely as well as one of the most complete of its kind, and includes a coverlet belonging to Archduke Albert and his wife Isabella.

A special collection in the complex of the Cinquantenaire Palace is **Autoworld** (open Apr–Sept Mon–Fri 9.30am–6pm, Sat–Sun 10am–6pm; Oct–Mar daily 9.30am–5pm; admission fee) which has an extensive collection of vintage cars that once belonged to prominent personalities.

Below: Belgian lace
Bottom: Greek sculpture

8B: WOLUWE & TERVUREN

After Cinquantenaire Park, Avenue Kennedy becomes Avenue de Tervuren. Note the row of stylish townhouses on the right hand side of the road. This avenue, constructed in 1897, leads over Montgomery Square and across Leopold II Square to the east. It then turns southeast towards the neighbourhood of **Woluwe-Saint Pierre**.

On the left-hand side of the Avenue de Tervuren is the ★ **Brussels City Transport Museum** (open Apr–early Oct Sat, Sun and hols 1.30–7pm; admission fee). It has a collection of old-fashioned open-sided trams on which, at weekends, you can ride to Tervuren through the woods.

The road curves around the northern end of **Woluwe Park** (80ha/200 acres) ❻. After the park there is a right turn towards Val Duchesse Abbey. Those not wishing to visit the abbey should remain on the Avenue de Tervuren.

ABBEY OF THE RED CLOISTER

Boulevard du Souverain leads between Woluwe Park and the adjacent greens with more ponds south towards the **Val Duchesse Abbey** (Abbaye du Val Duchesse) ❻. This was once the home of the oldest Dominican congregation in the Low Countries. It was founded in the 13th century by Duchess Aleyde of Brabant. It was here, back in 1956, that the European experts worked out the text of the founding treaties of the Common Market and Euratom. Near the abbey is the Romanesque St Anne's chapel, dating from the 12th century.

The Val Duchesse Abbey is located in the community of Auderghem, close to its very active cultural centre. The **Abbey of the Red Cloister** (Abbaye du Rouge Cloître) ❻ is also located here, to the south of Chaussée de Tervuren, down a steep winding path. Here you can have a drink or a meal outside, look round the gardens and the artists' workshops and walk through the huge **Forêt de Soignes**, often described as Brussels' 'lung'. To continue on to Tervuren from the Val Duchesse Abbey, turn left from Boulevard du Souverain, just south of Rond Point Souverain,

Map on page 65

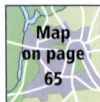

Old-timer trail
On weekends and public holidays from April to October, vintage trams trundle back and forth through the woods between the Brussels City Transport Museum and the Royal Museum of Central Africa.

Abbey of the Red Cloister, a good starting-point for a walk in the Soignes forest

onto Chaussée de Wavre. After a few hundred metres, turn left again onto the Chaussée de Tervuren. This merges with Avenue de Tervuren and leads to the town of Tervuren, about 14km (9 miles) away, which is on the road to Leuven.

Tervuren Castle ❻. The former domain of the dukes of Brabant was destroyed under orders from Joseph II. In its place, Leopold II built a château in Louis XVI style. Constructed between 1904–10, it was called the Museum of the Belgian Congo, a product of Leopold's grandiose colonial ambitions. The ★ **castle park**, 200ha (495 acres) of grounds with beautifully laid-out French-style gardens containing the tiny St Hubertus chapel, the 18th-century castle stables and the Gordael mill.

Brussels' huge forest lies to the southeast of the city

AFRICAN MUSEUM

The former colonial museum is today known as the ★ **Royal Museum of Central Africa** (Musée Royal de l'Afrique Centrale;open Tues–Fri

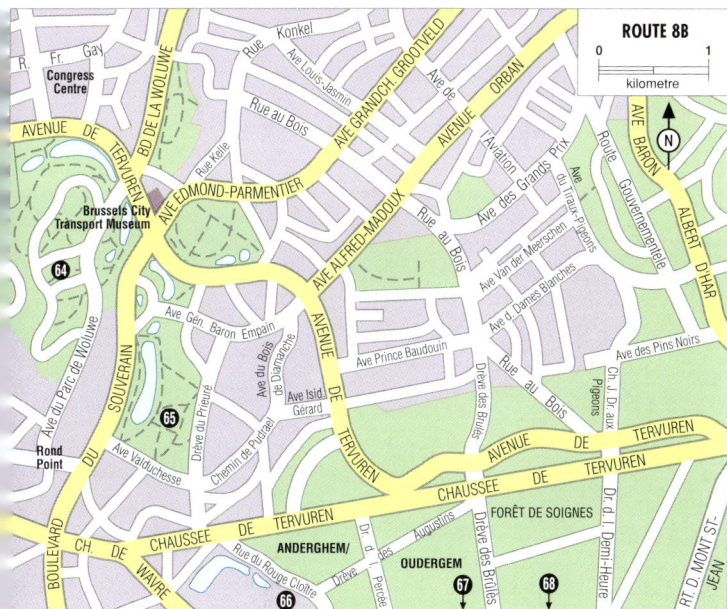

Map on page 65

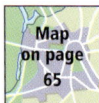

Famous first words
In the Royal Museum of Central Africa are several mementos of the journalist Henry Morton Stanley, who is perhaps best known for his greeting, 'Dr Livingstone, I presume', when he caught up with the famous explorer in the Belgian Congo.

10am–5pm, Sat–Sun 10am–6pm; admission fee). The entrance is at Leuvensesteenweg 13. The extensive collections, which were accumulated during Belgium's notorious period of colonial rule, relate in most part to the people of the Central African region – anthropology, history and ethnology – as well as to the natural history of Central Africa.

RIXENSART CASTLE

Just as Routes 8a and 8b can be combined to make a day's outing, it is also possible to travel to Tervuren and from there venture into the countryside. Jezus-Eik is a pretty village (with an excellent traditional bistro called Istas) which can be reached on foot or by bike through the Forêt de Soignes. Or follow the motorway about 15km (9 miles), to the Battlefield of Waterloo *(see Route 9, page 69).*

Another possibility is to take the motorway towards Namur for about the same distance, exiting at Rosières. From there it is about 3km (2 miles) south to **Rixensart Castle** ⑱ (open Apr–Sep Sun and public hols 2–6pm). Its buildings were constructed in the 17th century, in the elaborate style of the times and are full of beautiful furniture and tapestries.

Gardens of the Royal Museum of Central Africa

9: Southern Brussels

**Museums in Ixelles and Southern Brussels –
Abbey of La Cambre – Bois de la Cambre Woods
– Free University – Waterloo – Beersel Castle**

The route to the main destination of this tour, Bois
de la Cambre, south of the city centre, leaves the
boulevard ring at Place Louise on Avenue Louise.
To visit one or more of the museums described
below, you should proceed from Porte de Namur
along Chaussée de Wavre, making a detour
through the neighbourhood of Ixelles by car or
public transport.

On the left (Chaussée de Wavre 150), is the
Camille Lemonnier Museum (Musée Camille
Lemonnier) ❻❾ (open Mon 10am–noon, Wed and
Fri 10am–noon and 2–6pm; free). It contains
numerous documents from the literary life of this
French-Belgian author who was born in Ixelles
in 1845 and died there in 1913. He was patron
of the Jeune Belgique Group; his novels describe
the life of Belgian workers and peasants in a natural as well as socio-critical style. Continue on
Chaussée de Wavre turning left into Rue Vau-
tier. At house No 62 is the **Wiertz Museum** ❼❿
(open Tues–Fri and every other weekend
10am–noon and 1–5pm; free). This is the former atelier of the Belgian Romantic painter
Antoine Wiertz (1806–65) and contains most of
his works, many with morbid contents and some
with pan-optical effects.

INSTITUTE OF NATURAL SCIENCES

Across from the Wiertz Museum, in Leopold Park,
is the ★★ **Institute of Natural Sciences** (Institut des
Sciences Naturelles) ❼❶ (open Tues–Fri 9.30am–
4.45pm, Sat–Sun 10am–6pm; admission fee),
whose Zoology, Palaeontology and Mineralogy
sections are very popular with children. Chaussée
de Wavre makes a sharp right curve at Place Jourdan, heading southeast. At this point the route turns
right into Rue Gray. There is a fork to the right
onto Rue du Sceptre which leads across Raymond
Blykaerts Square to Rue Malibran.

Star Attraction
• Institute of
Natural Sciences

*Below: Abbey of La Cambre
and its tranquil gardens*

Map below

IXELLES MUSEUMS

At Rue Jan Van Volsem 71, the road parallel to Rue Malibran, is the ★ **Museum of Fine Arts of Ixelles** (Musée des Beaux-Arts d'Ixelles) **72** (open Tues–Fri 1–6.30pm, Sat–Sun 10am–5pm; admission fee). The museum contains mainly paintings by French and Belgian Impressionists. Go back along Chaussée de Vleurgat to the Avenue Louise. Crossing over the wide boulevard takes you to the **Constantin Meunier Museum 73** on your left at Rue de l'Abbaye 59. This house was built by the artist (1831–1905) at the end of the last century and contains about 170 of his sculptures and 120 of his oils, watercolours and drawings.

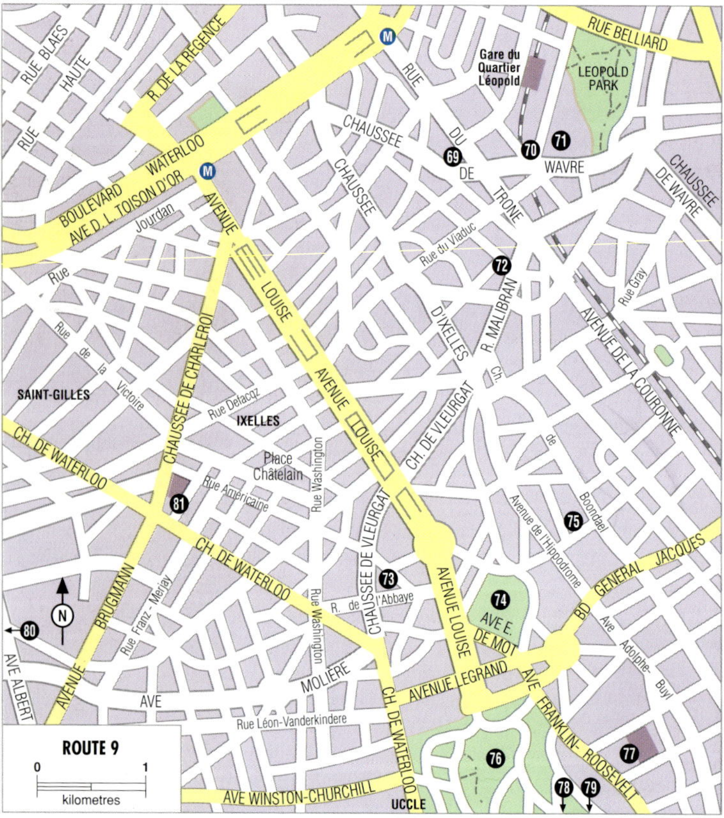

ROUTE 9

0 _____ 1

kilometres

Shortly before the end of Avenue Louis, at the northern edge of the wooded Bois de la Cambre on the left, is the **Abbey of La Cambre** (Abbaye de la Cambre) **㊲**. The tranquil gardens, which are laid out on five different levels, form an oasis of calm in an otherwise busy part of town. Today the abbey houses a college of Decorative Arts.

A short walk from the Abbey is the **Children's Museum** (Musée des Enfants) **㊵** at Rue du Bourgemestre 15 (open July Mon–Fri 2.30–5pm; Sept–June Mon, Wed and school hols (except public hols and Sun May–June) 2.30–5pm; admission fee). The wooded park of **Bois de la Cambre** **㊶** is about 500m (1,640ft) wide, 2km (1.2 miles) long and encompasses about 100ha (250 acres). It is one tiny corner of the huge Soignes Woods (Forêt de Soignes) which lies to the southeast of the city, and is a very popular place for strolling and lying in the sun. The small De Poche Theatre is here in Châlet du Gymnase. On the eastern side of the park is a complex of buildings housing the **Free University of Brussels** (Université Libre de Bruxelles) **㊷**, founded in 1834.

WATERLOO

On the western edge of Bois de la Cambre, Chaussée de Waterloo leads south from the Soignes Woods to the ★★**Waterloo Battlefield** **㊸**, located about 20km (12 miles) from the city centre *(see Map, page 74)*. It was here in June 1815 that Napoleon suffered his crushing defeat at the hands of the English, Prussians and Dutch under the command of the Duke of Wellington and Marshal Blücher. To be precise, the actual battle took place a few kilometres further south at Belle Alliance, but the victorious generals waged their campaign from this point. The almost 40-m (130-ft) high Lion's Hill (Butte du Lion; open daily Apr–Sept 9.30am–6.30pm, Oct–Mar 10am–5pm; admission fee; visitor centre free) is crowned by a cast iron monument of a lion.

At the foot of the hill, in Braine l'Alleud, is an interesting **Panorama Museum** (open daily

Abbey grounds
The Abbey of La Cambre commemorates a Cistercian brotherhood founded here in the 13th century, in the middle of the Soignes Woods. Particularly interesting are the late 14th-century Gothic church and the cloisters which were restored in 1934. The abbey seen here today, built in the 18th century under the direction of the Abbess Séraphine de Snoy, is surrounded by lovely French-style gardens.

Lion's Hill, Waterloo

Map
on page
68

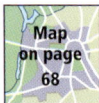

Beersel castle
Instead of heading directly back to the city, you could pay a visit to **Beersel Castle** ⑦⑨ *(see Map, page 51).* This castle, with its three unusual-shaped towers, dates from the early 14th century and is surrounded by a wide moat. After a siege at the end of the 15th century, the castle was partially rebuilt, then restored in 1920. Nearby Huisingen is ideal for children, with its golf course and amusement park.

Art nouveau at the Horta Museum

Apr–Sept 9.30am–6.30pm, Oct–Mar 10am–5pm; admission fee; visitor centre free) of the battle. Numerous historic buildings are also preserved, including the Inn of Belle Alliance where Napoleon had his headquarters. A museum is housed in an old inn which served as headquarters for the Duke of Wellington.

The return trip to Brussels leads either via the motorway or via the road from Alsemberg. Two more sights lie along this route. At the end of the motorway is the **Abbey of St-Denis** (Abbaye de St-Denis) ⑧⓪. There are only a few remains of the original 18th-century abbey, but beside them is the 11th-century church of St-Denis, a fine example of the Gothic style.

HORTA MUSEUM

The road from Alsemberg, the Chaussée d'Alsemberg, leads to the southernmost point of the boulevard ring (Porte de Hal). However, it is also possible to turn right beforehand onto Avenue Brugmann, making a short detour. Just off Chaussé de Waterloo is the ★★ **Horta Museum** ③① (open Tues–Sun 2–5.30pm; admission fee). The entrance is at 25 Rue Américaine. Victor Horta (1861–1947) was the father of Belgian art nouveau, and this is one of his houses, full of beautiful furniture, natural light and flowing, sensuous lines.

10: Western Brussels

Basilica of the Sacred Heart in Koekelberg – Groot Bijgaarden Castle – Gaasbeek Castle – Erasmus House

The sights in the western part of Brussels are considerably more spread out than those in the other three outlying sectors of the city. Nevertheless, for those who have time, they are certainly well worth a visit. This is particularly true of the basilica of Koekelberg and the Erasmus House. The route to Koekelberg is easy to find. Leave the boulevard ring at Place Sainctelette and drive along Boulevard Léopold II towards Ghent and Ostend. In the western part of Elisabeth Park this road divides, passing on either side of the ★**National Basilica of the Sacred Heart** (Basilique Nationale du Sacré Coeur) **82** in Koekelberg. It serves as a memorial to all the heroes who gave their lives for their fatherland. Leopold II laid the cornerstone of this 162-m (531-ft) long structure in 1905, but it wasn't until 1970 that the finishing touches were applied. Said to be one of the largest churches in the world, its modern architecture and lovely stained-glass windows are particularly noteworthy.

Below: Groot Bijgaarden
Bottom: National Basilica

GROOT BIJGAARDEN

Beyond the basilica, the route leaves the E5 motorway to the left via Avenue du Panthéon, turning right at Avenue Josse Goffin. This turns into Avenue du Roi Albert, which leads through the neighbourhood of Berchem-Sainte Agathe to the town of Groot Bijgaarden. From here, it follows Brusselsestraat to the **Castle of Groot Bijgaarden** (Kasteel van Groot Bijgaarden) **83**, located 7km (4 miles) from the city centre. This castle dates from the 16th and 17th century and was completely restored in 1922 by its owners, the Pelgrim family. Because it is still a private residence, it is not open to the public. The castle museum is well appointed with Renaissance furniture as well as a collection of paintings by old German and Italian Masters.

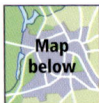

GAASBEEK CASTLE

Another attractive castle is located about 10km (6 miles) further south of here. The route to this castle leads over many small unmarked roads, through Sint-Martens-Bodegem, across Highway No 9 east of Schepdaal and then into Gaasbeek. The **Castle of Gaasbeek** (Kasteel van Gaasbeek) ❽❹, originally dating from the 13th century, has been renovated on numerous occasions throughout the years. It has a splendid collection of tapestries, silverware and furniture.

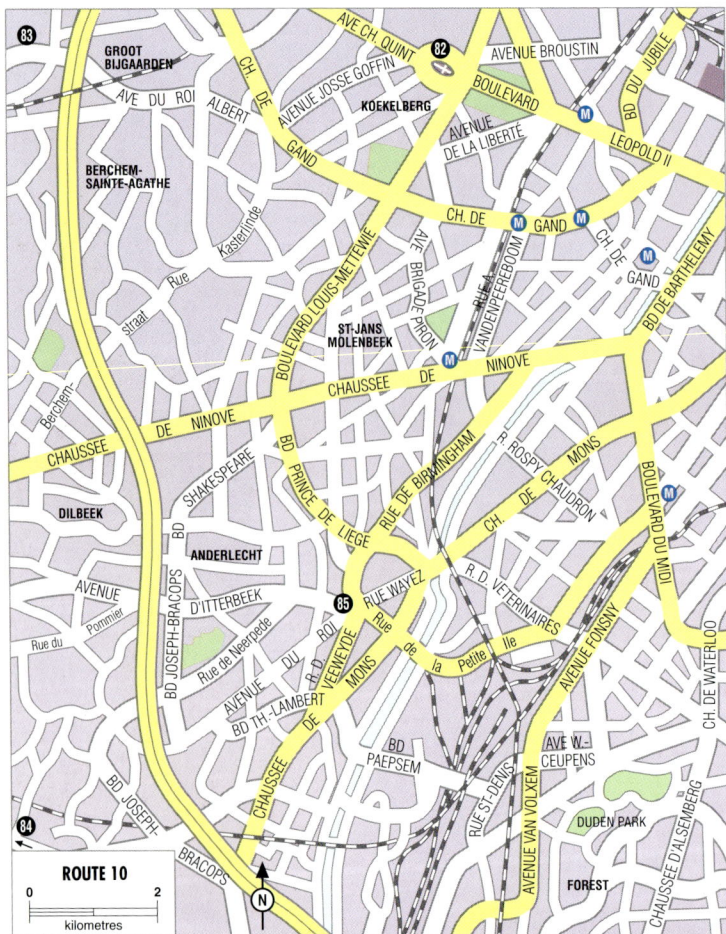

Map below

ROUTE 10
0   2
kilometres

ANDERLECHT

The return route to the centre of Brussels leads first to the city limits via Route de Lennik and then through Anderlecht, the largest community in the southwest of Greater Brussels, straddling both sides of the Charleroi Canal. It follows Chaussée de Mons about 1km further north to Rue de Veeweide on the left.

This leads to the two squares of Place de la Vaillance and Square Jef-Dillen. Here, almost adjacent to one another, are the Erasmus House and the church of St Peter and St Guido ㉟. Nearby, in Rue de Chapelein 1–7, is the Anderlecht Cultural Centre (Centre Intellectuel).

ERASMUS HOUSE

The ★ **Erasmus House** (Maison d'Erasme) in Rue de Chapitre 31 (open Tues–Sun 10am–5pm; admission fee) presents an interesting cross-section of the life and works of Erasmus of Rotterdam (1466–1536), who is today generally recognised as the greatest Humanist of his age. It was here in this 15th-century, red-brick patrician house that Erasmus lodged during his five-month visit to Brussels in 1521; it belonged to a canon and friend of his named Pierre Wichman.

The rooms, adorned with valuable paintings, give a good idea of the original furnishings of the period. Well worth seeing is Erasmus's study, which contains his desk, his armchair, and even his inkwell, books and original manuscripts. His reliquary holds his death mask and his private seal. The various paintings on the walls are ascribed to the artists Quentin Metsys, Albrecht Dürer and Hans Holbein.

The church of **St Peter and St Guido** (Eglise Sts-Pierre-et-Guidon), a Gothic structure with a Romanesque crypt, was constructed between the 14th and 16th centuries. It has a belfry and some magnificent frescoes.

From here, the return route follows Rue Wayez, which links up with the Chaussée de Mons after having crossed over the canal at E.van de Velde Square.

Missing Brussels
The humanist philosopher Desiderius Erasmus taught at the University of Leuven from 1516 to 1521, and lived in that town and in Anderlecht, which was then a village outside Brussels. He missed the city, and the province of Brabant in general. In a letter from Basle, bemoaning his distance from the province, he wrote: 'Would that I were closer to Brabant.'

The writing desk of Erasmus of Rotterdam

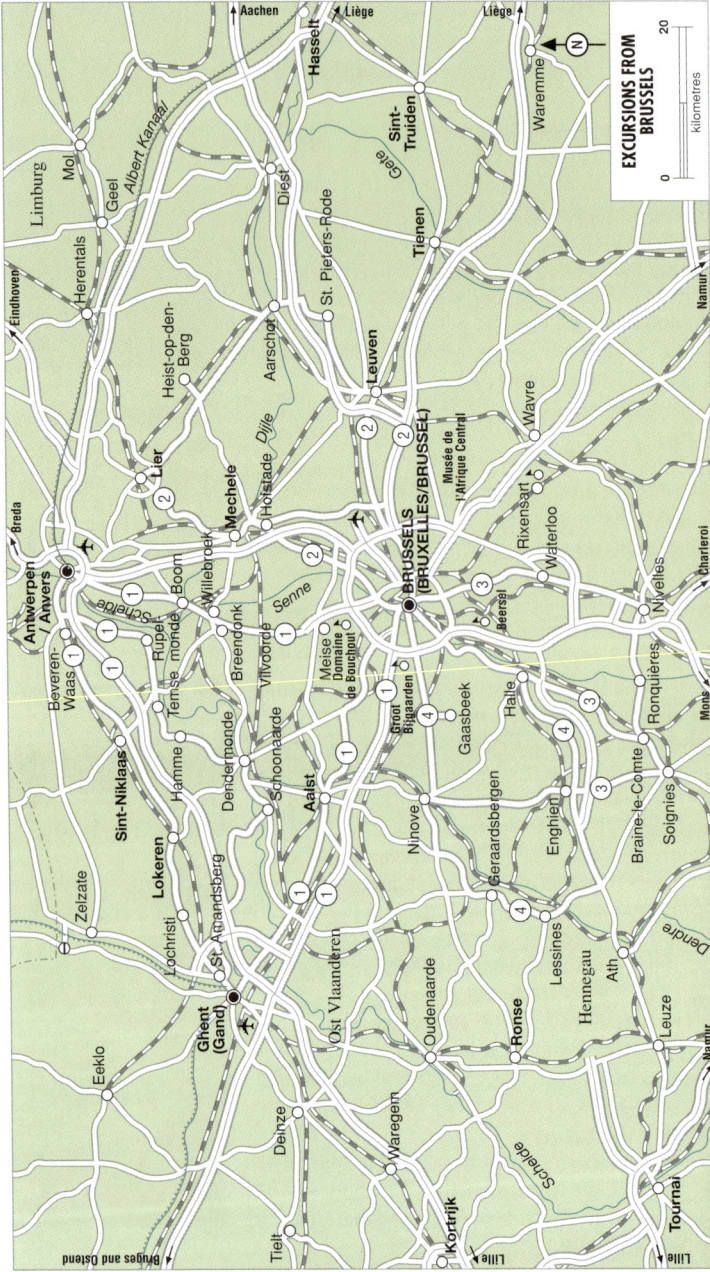

EXCURSIONS FROM BRUSSELS

0   20

kilometres

Excursion 1: Antwerp–Ghent

Antwerp – Sint-Niklaas – Lokeren – Rupelmonde – Ghent – Aalst (170km/105 miles)

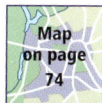

Map on page 74

The central location of the Belgian capital makes it an ideal starting point for both long and short excursions into all parts of the country. We have limited their selection to a zone of 50km (30 miles) around Brussels, suggesting sights that can be reached easily on a day trip.

The first excursion heads north and northwest through Flemish Brabant to the Flemish provinces of Antwerp and East Flanders. Rather than taking the main thoroughfare to Antwerp via Mechelen (this city is covered in Excursion 2, *see page 84*), the route suggested here is via Vilvoorde-Breendonk-Boom *(see Map, page74)*. This provides the opportunity to visit the baroque abbey church of Grimbergen west of Vilvoorde as well as the Domein Bouchout in Meise, both of which are described in Route 7 *(see page 53)*.

Breaking contact

Until 1995, there was just one Belgian province of Brabant (Holland has a province called North Brabant). But in that year the proud old province was carved up along the line of Belgium's language divide. There's now a Flemish Brabant in the north and a Walloon Brabant in the south, giving the country 10 provinces.

FORT BREENDONK

This route leaves Brussels on the N1, travelling alongside the Canal de Willebroek, also known as the Sea Canal. It leads mainly through industrialised regions before turning left in Vilvoorde onto the N211. This leads via Grimbergen to the A12 north of Meise. This motorway can, of course, also be taken directly from Brussels. About 10km (6 miles) north from Meise is the town of **Breendonk**. The town's fort served as a concentration camp and an estimated 3,500 prisoners passed through here. It was converted to a national museum (open daily 9.30am–5.30pm, closed last Sun of Aug, Dec 25, Jan 1; admission fee) in 1948. To visit the museum, follow the signs to Fort Breendonk (not to the town of Breendonk).

Just past Breendonk is Willebroek, the town which gave the canal its name. The next town, Boom is the centre of the Rupel region and, with its clay-rich soil, Belgium's most important brick region. The canal joins the Rupel river here.

Street performer in Antwerp

Map on page 74

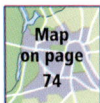

Steen scene
The most noteworthy sight on the outskirts of the city is the **Steen**, on the banks of the Scheldt, a castle which houses the ★ **Maritime Museum** (Nationaal Scheepvaartmuseum; open Tues–Sun 10am–4.45pm; admission fee). The oldest parts of this fortress date from the 9th century while the rest was built in 1225. The departure point for ships which take visitors on tours of the harbour is near the castle.

Cathedral of Our Dear Lady

ANTWERP (ANTWERPEN/ANVERS)

The vibrant and prosperous capital of the province of ★★ **Antwerp** is situated 50km (31 miles) north of Brussels and has a population of about 500,000 (680,000 including the suburbs). Although Antwerp is almost 90km (55 miles) from the open sea, it is Belgium's most important port; the harbour is on the Scheldt river. The delightful old town, on the east banks of the river Scheldt (Schelde), is surrounded by a 6-km (4-mile) long boulevard built in 1859 to replace the 16th-century Spanish city wall. Almost all of the sights of interest are located in this part of Antwerp.

THE CATHEDRAL

The best place to begin a tour of the city centre is at the Late Gothic ★ **Meat Hall** (Vleeshuis), built in the 16th century to serve as a butchers' market hall and guild hall. The butchers' meeting room is particularly interesting. Today the building houses a local museum (open Tues–Sun 10am–5pm; admission fee) with archaeological finds and artistic crafts. It is just a short distance from here to the **Grote Markt** with the Town Hall (Stadhuis), built in 1561–5 in Renaissance style. Inside there are some interesting murals depicting the history of the city.

In Gildekamersstraat, which leads off the square, is the **Museum of Folklore** (Volkskunde-museum; open Tues–Sun 10am–5pm; admission fee), founded in 1907, which provides an extensive overview of the folk art of Flanders. The ★★ **Cathedral of Our Lady** (Onze-Lieve-Vrouwekerk) is south of the museum, on Handschoenmarkt. It is Belgium's largest Gothic church, as well as being one of the biggest Gothic churches in the world. Construction was begun in the early 14th century but was not completed until the 17th century. The impressive interior contains works by Rubens as well as spectacular stained-glass windows and a carillon with 47 chimes. The largest bell, that with the deepest tone, weighs 8 tons. From the cathedral, the tour leads through Korte Nieuwstraat to Hendrik Conscienceplein with its ★ **St Carolus Borromeuskerk**, built in 17th-century baroque style. The church, which possesses a lovely facade as well as elegant steeples, was damaged by fire in 1718. The Rubens Chapel, however, was spared from the flames. A wealth of art treasures and a collection of old lace can be seen in the museum.

THE JEWISH QUARTER

The tour now returns to Korte Nieuwstraat and continues along Lange Nieuwstraat leading to the Burgundian chapel which dates from the 15th century; its arches and murals are striking. Just a bit further along the same street is the Late Gothic (15th/16th-century) ★ **Sint-Jakobskerk** with its unfinished steeple. Its interior is decorated with a wide variety of art treasures including sculptures, paintings, crafted objects of silver and gold, embroidery, manuscripts and robes. The Rubens' burial chapel is situated in the choir.

Continuing along Nieuwstraat, the route crosses the broad ring boulevard at Franklin Rooseveltplein. This boulevard was built along the lines of the former city wall. To the right, on Lange Herentalsestraat is the **Provincial Diamond Museum** (Provinciaal Diamant-museum; open Apr–Oct Mon–Sat 9.30am–5.30pm, Sun and hols 10am–5pm; Nov–Mar

Star Attraction
• **Cathedral of Our Lady**

Below: Steen Maritime Museum
Bottom: Grote Markt, with a statue of Brabo, Antwerp's legendary hero

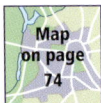

Map on page 74

Zoo times
Behind the Jewish quarter is **Antwerp Zoo** (open daily Dec–Jan 10am–4.30pm; Feb and Oct 16–Nov 10am–4.45pm; Mar 1–15 and Oct 1–15 10am–5.15pm; Mar 16–June and Sept 10am–5.45pm; July–Aug 10am–6.15pm; admission fee) with its Museum of Natural History, planetarium, aquarium, delphinarium, nocturama (with nocturnal animals), aviary and reptile house.

Mon–Sat 9.30am–5.30pm; free, except for special events) where a display depicts a diamond's progress from mining to the finished jewel or industrial diamond. This is the heart of the Jewish quarter, where you will see many Orthodox Jews in traditional dress, and a it is good place to buy diamond jewellery.

RUBENS HOUSE

Next to the zoo is the grand 19th-century railway station, the Centraal Station. Following Keyserlei and Frankrijklei, the route leads via Leysstraat to the broad connecting street of the Meir. Just off this street is ★★**Rubens House** (Rubenshuis; open Tues–Sun 10am–4.45pm; admission fee), the artist's home until his death in 1640. Aside from the magnificently appointed interior housing ten works by Rubens, the house has an impressive portico, which makes an appearance in many of his pictures. Many more of his paintings can be enjoyed in the **Royal Museum of Fine Arts** on Leopold de Waelplaats.

At the end of Rubensstraat, Schuttershofstraat leads to the right. Follow this to Lange Gasthuisstraat where the ★**Mayer van den Bergh Museum**, with one of Belgium's most important collections, is located. The *Dulle Griet* by Pieter Brueghel the Elder is the main attraction of the

Interior of Antwerp's St Carolus Borromeuskerk

collection of paintings. The museum houses a rich collection of sculptures from the 6th–18th century, gold and silver objects and lace and embroidery.

THE BIRD MARKET

On the same street, is the ★ **Maagdenhuis**, a museum with wonderful faience pieces from the 16th century and valuable paintings, sculptures, and other ornaments from the 15th century. If you go a little further down the Lange Gasthuisstraat with its attractive, historical facades, and then bear left, you'll come to the Oude Vaartplaats. This is where Antwerp's famous ★ **Bird Market** is held every Sunday morning, selling everything from animals, plants to food, clothing and art. In the evening the area is a popular meeting place. The **Beguine Convent**, on Rodestraat, is rarely visited by tourists, but this 16th-century group of alleyways, cottages and gardens is an oasis of peace and quiet amidst the bustling city.

*Below: Rubens House
Bottom: Rubens' Education of the Virgin in the Royal Museum of Fine Arts*

SOUTH TO GHENT

There are several different routes which lead from Antwerp south to Ghent. If you are short of time take the A14 motorway. If you have more time and want to become acquainted with the countryside follow the old Route 14 north of the motorway through Sint-Niklaas. Alternatively, take the small roads which follow the River Scheldt (Schelde). All of these routes cross the provincial border into East Flanders just a few kilometres west of Antwerp.

SINT-NIKLAAS

The first Flemish town along Route 14 is known as the Town of Lace, **Beveren-Waas**. Charming, tree-lined lanes lead to the Cortewalle Castle and the church with its richly decorated interior. It was built in the Scheldt Gothic style.

Sint-Niklaas (population 68,500) is the major town in the densely populated and fertile Waas region. Its huge main square is the location of the neo-Gothic Town Hall (1876) with a carillon in

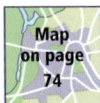

Map on page 74

Flower power

From the end of July until September, the aroma of flowers is in the air as the begonia fields which the Lochristi area is renowned for, spreading over 125ha (310 acres), come alive in a magnificent burst of colour.

Dendermonde's Grote Markt

the tower, the church of Sint-Niklaas, built in the 15th and 16th century and often restored and expanded in later years, as well as numerous other interesting buildings. One of these is the Parochiehuis, built in 1663 and originally used as a vicarage before being converted to the Town Hall. Today it houses the courts. Another of the buildings is the Ciperage, built in 1662 as a prison. Today it serves as the library. Behind the Town Hall is the towering church of Our Lady (Onze-Lieve-Vrouwekerk).

Lokeren (population 28,000) is 15km (9 miles) further, south of Route 14. The church of St Lawrence here has a carved pulpit dating from 1736. Twelve kilometres (7 miles) further is **Lochristi**, a town stretching along both sides of the road. The road continues on towards Ghent through Sint-Amandsberg whose cemetery is the last resting place of numerous prominent Flemish personalities from the world of art and science.

For those who select the southern route which leaves Antwerp via Burcht on the Scheldt, the following sights are of interest.

Rupelmonde is a centuries-old sailing and fishing village, and birthplace of the geographer Mercator. This famous 16th-century Belgian was held prisoner in the moated castle here. The tower still stands and a monument to Mercator stands in front of the church of St Mary (Mariakerk).

DENDERMONDE

The route now leads through the shipbuilding village of Temse with its wonderful eel specialities in the restaurants along the wharf. Next comes Hamme, where a swampy region called De Bunt, lying between the river and the Durme valley, contains a wealth of interesting flora and fauna. The route continues through **Dendermonde**, whose Palace of Justice tower is decorated by a bronze horse. The sights worth seeing in this town of 42,000 people include the Town Hall with its bell tower in the main square and the interior of the church of St Mary (Mariakerk) with its wealth of art treasures.

Continuing on through Schoonaarde and Overmere (site of a Museum of the Peasants' Revolt) and, via a short detour, through Laarne with its impressive moated castle, the road now leads to the capital of East Flanders, located just under 60km (37 miles) from Antwerp.

Star Attraction
•Ghent

GHENT (GENT)

In the Middle Ages, ★★ **Ghent** (current population 100,000, with suburbs 225,390) was the capital of the cloth trade. Today, it is still the textile and metal industry which makes Ghent an important commercial centre. Despite its inland location, the city is the country's second largest port owing to the canal link to the Westerschelde and thus to the North Sea. Numerous structures from past centuries are preserved in Ghent.

THE CITY CENTRE

The main attractions are concentrated in an almost circular area surrounding the Town Hall and the cloth hall. On the west side of the Botermarkt is the three-storey ★ **Town Hall** (Stadhuis) with a facade decorated with Doric, Ionic and Corinthian pillars.

Across from the Town Hall is the **Cloth Hall** (Lakenhalle; open mid-Mar to mid-Nov daily

Below: dishing up waterzooi, a Ghent speciality
Bottom: St Michael's Bridge

Map on page 74

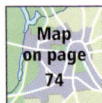

Missing brother?
It is not certain whether Jan van Eyck painted *The Adoration of the Mystic Lamb* alone or with his brother Hubert, who is cited in an enigmatic inscription. Many art historians believe it to be the work of Jan alone.

10am–1pm and 2–6pm; admission fee) built in 1425. The Belfry (Belfort) is 95m (310ft) high and dates from the 14th century. On the 5th storey is the carillon of Ghent, famous for its 'Klokke Roeland', a storm bell, and for its pure and harmonious sound. On the square in front of this building are the Youths Fountain and the Triumphante Bell.

Passing by the huge St Nicholas Church/Sint-Niklaaskerk (13th-century), the route leads to the Koornmarkt with a variety of houses dating from the 16th and 17th century. It then leads around the former central post office and to St Michael's Bridge, crossing over the Leie to **St Michael's Church** (Sint-Michielskerk), which was begun in 1440 and completed in the 17th century. Returning across the bridge towards the Koornmarkt, the path follows Graslei along the banks of the Leie.

Recrossing the Leie via Grasbrug, the route reaches the **Design Museum Ghent** (open Tues–Sun 10am–6pm; admission fee) in Jan Breydelstraat. Here, in an old patrician house, a rich collection, including period furniture, is on display.

'S GRAVENSTEEN

The route now turns to the right, crossing the Leie once again, and leading to one of the main attractions, the old castle fortress of the Counts of

The famous altarpiece of St Bavo's Cathedral

Flanders, ★ **'s Gravensteen** (open daily Apr– Sept 9am–6pm, Oct–Mar 9am–5pm; admission fee). Built between 1180 and 1200 on the foundation of a 10th-century structure, it was expanded and renovated numerous times over the years.

From Sint-Veerleplein the route crosses over the Leie bridge and Groentenmarkt, leading through Hoogpoort to the Town Hall. Anyone especially interested in church architecture might want to walk about 300m (985ft) down Borluutstraat to visit St Jacob's Church (Sint-Jakobskerk), completed in the 17th century. It has a Romanesque portal (12th-century) and a tabernacle dating from 1593. Also, behind the Cloth Hall, and a few steps down Sint-Baafsplein is ★★ **St Bavo's Cathedral** (Sint-Baafskathedraal), which was built between the 10th and 16th centuries. Its altarpiece, the *Adoration of the Holy Lamb* (1420–32) by Jan van Eyck, is number one of the 'seven wonders of Belgium' and is regarded as the greatest masterpiece of early Flemist art.

AALST

The 55-km (34-mile) return trip from Ghent to Brussels can be made via the A10 motorway linking Ostend to the capital. For those with a bit more time, however, an alternative route along the N9 is recommended, with a pause in **Aalst**. The entire excursion can be shortened by eliminating the trip to Ghent and heading south directly from Dendermonde *(see page 80)* to Aalst. This town (population 79,000) is situated on the River Dender and is famous both as an industrial city and as a centre for cut flowers. The interesting sights are grouped around the market place with its monument to Dirk Martens, who founded the first printing shop of the Low Countries here. In the interior courtyard of the Gothic Town Hall is a country house in rococo style, whose bell tower houses a carillon.

The road back to Brussels is lined on both sides with hills and hop fields. Passing through the small village of Hekelgem, note the two old windmills, both of which are historic preservation sites.

Star Attraction
• **St Bavo's Cathedral**

Below: gabled houses along the Korenlei
Bottom: 's Gravensteen castle

Map on page 74

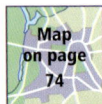

Camelot-on-the-Dijle
Between 1507 and 1530, Mechelen was the seat of Margaret of Austria, regent for the future Emperor Charles V. She sponsored a brilliant court culture by patronising prominent artists, musicians and scholars, among them Erasmus.

Gabled houses along the Korenlei

Excursion 2: Mechelen–Leuven

Mechelen – Lier – Aarschot – Leuven (115km/ 71 miles)

Just as in the first excursion, this route leads north from Brussels, either along the A1 motorway (E19) or the N1 towards Antwerp. It exits, however, at Mechelen-Zuid. If you choose the N1, make a stop at the national domain of Hofstade, a recreational centre with several ponds and sandy beaches. Two larger lakes provide opportunities for a variety of water sports. The park also contains a bird sanctuary.

MECHELEN

This town of 76,000 inhabitants is presided over by the 97-m (318-ft) high Gothic steeple of ★ **St Rombout's Cathedral** (good panorama). The steeple, begun in 1452 and completed in 1578, was originally designed to reach a height of 168m (551ft). It turned into a colossal stump, however, when William of Orange appropriated the necessary building materials for the construction of the Willemstad fortress. The tower has one of Belgium's most beautiful carillons, with 49 bells. The cathedral itself was built mainly in the 13th and 14th century; its interior is in baroque style. It houses the renowned painting by Van Dyck, *Christ on the Cross* (1627), the tombs of two cardinals, a baroque statue of the first archbishop of Mechelen, Cardinal Granvella and the burial chapel of Cardinal Mercier (1851–1926).

The focal point of the city is the **Grote Markt**, lined with Renaissance and baroque houses. On the south side is the **Cloth Hall** (Lakenhalle), modelled on that in Bruges and dating from the 14th century. Here, too, is the former Schepenhuis (city council building), today the Town Hall. Another important building, to the east of the Grote Markt, is the Palace of Justice. This was once the residence of the city ruler, Margaret of Austria, as well as of Cardinal Granvella. The building was constructed in 1503–7. Its Renaissance facade was fashioned between 1517–26.

Also in Mechelen is the 15th-century **St John's Church** with an important altarpiece by Rubens, *The Adoration of the Magi*. In the southern part of the city, the Brussels Gate with its double tower is the only remaining one of the 12 city gates.

Star Attraction
•Lier

LIER

The tour continues north via Duffel (the town that gave us the thick wool cloth for duffle coats), where it crosses the Nete, to ★★ **Lier**. This picturesque town was popularised by the writings of Felix Timmerman (1886–1947), whose novels depicting traditional Flemish life have been translated into many languages. Sights of note here are the 18th-century Town Hall with a bell tower from 1369, the oldest Beguine convent in the Netherlands, and the **Zimmer** or **Cornelius Tower**. The tower, originally a part of the city wall, got its name from the Lier watchmaker and astronomer Louis Zimmer, the creator of the tower's amazing clock. Although only 13 dials are visible from outside, inside the tower a further 57 dials show the time in every part of the world, as well as astronomical phenomena, such as the phases of the moon and the path of the stars.

The late-Gothic structure of St Gommarus is also noteworthy. Its 80-m (260-ft) high tower, with carillon, is said to have the shape of a pepper-mill.

Below: Lier's amazing astronomical clock
Bottom: St Rombout's Cathedral, Mechelen

Map on page 74

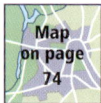

Stella Artois
Beer has been brewed in Leuven since 1366. The master brewer in 1708 was one Sebastian Artois, whose descendants carried on his trade for many years. In 1926 a special Christmas beer was created, designed to be as clear as a star in the winter sky - and Stella Artois was born. The brewery just outside the town now produces about 9 million hectolitres (198 million gallons) of beer every year.

Students in the university town of Leuven

Aarschot is the next destination on the route. The old ducal grain mills, the church of St Mary's, a Gothic masterpiece, and the Beguine convent are of interest here.

LEUVEN/LOUVAIN

This pleasant city of 88,000 residents was an important European textile centre in the 13th and 14th centuries. Additionally, a university was founded here in 1425. Although the city was severely damaged during World War II, the market place's two main attractions, the Late Gothic Town Hall and St Peter's Church, did not suffer any lasting effects.

The ★★**Town Hall** (Stadhuis) was built between 1448–63 for the ruling Duke of Burgundy With its towers, arched windows and spectacularly moulded facade, this building is a beautiful example of medieval architecture. The detached facades are composed of three storeys of Gothic arched windows. On the four corners and above the front and rear gables, six slender towers protrude like the masts of a ship. The elaborate reliefs depict biblical scenes.

St Peter's Church/Sint-Pieterskerk is also a late-Gothic structure (begun in 1425). Its exterior was never completed because the ground on which it stands was too soft and the west steeple was therefore never built. Within the church, the 12-m (39-ft) high sanctuary as well as the rood screen (1450) were executed by Mathieu de Layens, the architect who also designed the Town Hall. The most valuable treasures inside the church, however, are the two paintings by Dirk Bouts, who lived in Leuven and died there in 1475. These are the *Martyrdom of St Erasmus* and his masterpiece, created between 1464–8 for the sacrament chapel, *The Last Supper Altar*.

Not far away is **Oude Markt**, a busy cobbled square lined with bars and restaurants, and the scene of a market every Friday.

From Leuven it is about 25km (16 miles) back to Brussels either along the A3 motorway, the N2 (via Zaventem) or the N3 via Tervuren.

Excursion 3: Nivelles–Halle

Nivelles – Ronquières – Soignies – Halle (95km/ 59 miles)

Excursions 3 and 4 both lead south and southwest, which means that they can be combined easily into one longer excursion. Leaving Brussels on the N5, the route heads south towards Waterloo, continuing on the N27 past the Lion's Mound. On the right side, just before reaching the city, is the race track of Nivelles-Baulers (Autodrome).

NIVELLES

★ **Nivelles** (population 22,000) was one of Belgium's most picturesque historic cities, before it was badly damaged during World War II. It grew up around a nuns' abbey and was, until the 17th century, one of the cloth cities of Belgium.

The **abbey** in question is dedicated to **St Gertrude**. Founded in the 7th century, it is the oldest such establishment in Belgium. According to legend, following the death of the Frankish ruler Pepin the Elder, his widow Itta retired with their daughter Gertrude to a villa on the hillside overlooking the Thines Valley. After the death of her mother and a deteriorating marriage to Dagobert I, Gertrude founded the monastery, at the instigation of Amand, Bishop of Maastricht.

Star Attraction
• **Leuven's Town Hall**

Below: Leuven's Town Hall
Bottom: St Gertrude's cloisters

Map
on page
74

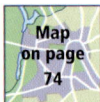

Remains of the day
On the Sunday after St Michael's day, Nivelles is the scene of a procession during which the remains of St Gertrude are carried 12km (7 miles) through the city and surrounding area. This tradition has been preserved since the 12th century.

Immediately she set about ordering books from Rome and summoned monks from Ireland. Nowadays, the abbey church, which dates from the 11th century, is regarded as one of the finest Romanesque churches in the country. It consists of a main nave and two aisles, separated from each other by square and cruciform pillars. It was destroyed by fire in 1940 but was reconstructed in its 12th-century form. The porch is flanked by two small towers, the Tour Madame and the Tour de Jean de Nivelles. The copper figure of Jean de Nivelles on the right steeple strikes the time and has become the city's landmark. It was donated by the Duke of Burgundy, Charles the Bold. The cloisters date from the 13th century. Reliefs depicting incidents in the life of Samson, including a scene in which Delilah is cuttting his hair, adorn the North door. The South portal contains a statue of the archangel Michael with outspread wings.

Apart from the abbey, the church and monastery of St Francis, as well as the Museum of Antiquities and the Dodaine Park are all worth a visit.

LOCK OF RONQUIERES

The route continues west from Nivelles along the N49 to an especially fascinating sight for any-

*Soignies: Collégiale
St Vincent*

one interested in technology. This is the ★★ **Boat lift of Ronquières** at the Lock of Ronquières on the Charleroi-Brussels Canal (daily 10am–7pm; tel: 065-36 04 64). This lift for barges of up to 1,350 tons went into operation here in 1968. It can lift or lower barges 68m (223ft) in one step. The barge drives into a steel lock measuring 90m (295ft) in length and 12m (39ft) in width. The lock, on 236 wheels, is pulled up (or let down) an incline measuring 1,430m (4,692ft) in length. The entire process takes 25 minutes and can be observed from the street bridge. An even better observation point, however, is from the 125-m (410-ft) high control tower (which fortunately has a lift). This construction, which replaced 28 locks, reduces from 35 to 14 hours the time a ship needs to travel the 70km (43 miles) between Charleroi and Brussels.

*Below: St Vincent's church
Bottom: welcome to Soignies*

SOIGNIES

Further west is Braine-le-Comte with a church dating from the 13th–16th century and a Renaissance Town Hall. Continuing another 7km (4 miles), the route reaches **Soignies** (population 23,400) with the cloister church of St Vincent. The cloister was donated by St Vincent, husband of St Waltraut, in 653. The only part of the original complex still surviving is the early Romanesque church (10th–11th century). The altar of this church contains a shrine with the earthly remains of Saint Vincent. His head is in another shrine in the choir. Soignies is also the scene of a procession, every Pentecost Sunday, which winds its way along 15km (9 miles). The city is noted for its nearby bluestone quarry, which provides the material to construct many buildings in the Low Countries.

From Soignies, two alternatives present themselves. One is to take the N57 north for 12km (7 miles) to Enghien when Excursion 4 can be joined. The other is to return to Brussels via **Halle**, described in Excursion 4 *(page 90)*. From here a short detour will lead to the moated Beersel Castle (described in *Route 9, page 70*).

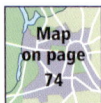

Map on page 74

Excursion 4: Halle–Ninove

Halle – Enghien/Edingen – Lessines – Geraardsbergen – Ninove (100km/62 miles)

This, the last excursion, can easily be combined with Excursion 3, as mentioned above *(see Map, page 74)*. The city of **Halle** is a bit less than 20km (12 miles) from the centre of Brussels. It can be reached either by leaving the motorway A7/E19 (towards Mons) at the Halle exit or via the N6. If taking the motorway, it is also possible to get off one exit earlier, in **Huizingen**, which has a magnificent gardens displaying over 1,200 species of plants, a golf course and an amusement park, ideal for entertaining small children.

HALLE

Halle, which is very close to the Flemish/ Walloon linguistic border, has a Gothic Basilica of Our Lady, a Flemish Renaissance Town Hall (Stadhuis) dating from 1616, with a bell tower and a baroque former Jesuit college. The latter now serves as the town's cultural centre and tourist information office. The ★ **Basilica of Our Lady**, built in 1341–1467, is a fine example of Brabant Gothic architecture, and has an extensive collection of interesting sculptures.

BILINGUAL ENGHIEN

Continuing along the N8 from Halle, the route leads west and soon crosses the boundary between the provinces of Walloon Brabant and Hainaut. The bilingual town of **Enghien** (population 4,500) lies directly on this boundary. The castle of the dukes of Enghien, destroyed during the French Revolution, was located in the park of the dukes of Arenberg. The park, which is open to the public, stretches across 324ha (800 acres) and contains numerous busts and statues. The alabaster tomb of the Archbishop of Toledo, Wilhelm von Croy, an important work of the Renaissance era, is found in the Capuchin monastery church.

Enghien town centre and park

From Enghien you can shorten this excursion (by about 20km/12 miles) by driving directly north to Ninove along the N255 or by following the route described in Excursion 3 in the opposite direction, on the N55, which can be reached in Soignies. Otherwise, continue along the N7 to Bassily. From here a small road leads to **Lessines** on the Dender. A narrow, winding road leads from the market place to a lovely square lined with linden trees. This is the site of the church which has four aisles in addition to the nave. Nearby is the museum of the Notre Dame à la Rose, with its marvellous collection of copper and wrought-iron works.

NINOVE

The route now leads northeast through the Dender valley, sometimes approaching the river, sometimes meandering away from it. The next town is **Geraardsbergen** where a replica of the Brussels Manneken-Pis is found on the outdoor steps of the Town Hall (with four corner towers).

Ninove, also situated on the banks of the Dender, is the final stop on this excursion. The Koepoort Gate is a remnant of the city wall. The Church of St Mary has a baroque interior with monumental confessionals and wood panelling. On the return trip to Brussels, it is possible to make a detour to Gaasbeek Castle *(see page 72)*.

Below: Geraardsbergen from above
Bottom: the Church of St Mary in Ninove

Architecture

It was not until the 12th and 13th century, when it began to thrive commercially, amid a flourish of building activity, that the city of Brussels really began to develop its own art and culture.

Europe's most skilled sculptors and artists, masons and architects, were employed to adorn Brussels, and their achievements are preserved in the city's buildings. One of the prime examples is the Gothic cathedral of St Michael. Construction was begun in 1226 and continued for several centuries. Among the secular Gothic structures in Brussels, nowhere are the mason's skills better reflected than in the 15th-century Town Hall. The left wing and the lower section of the tower were built between 1402–20. The tower, which soars to a height of 91 metres (291ft) above the Grand' Place, was built between 1449–55. From 1515, work continued on the King's House opposite. Most of the buildings on the Grand' Place were reconstructed with splendid baroque facades after the French bombardment of 1695.

More benign French influence on the city included the construction by Barnabé Guimard of the church of St James on the Coudenberg in 1776 and the Palace of the Council of Brabant (1778–83), which later became the parliament building. Renaissance and neoclassical architecture is best evidenced in Brussels by the buildings around Place Royale, the Stock Exchange and the Palace of Justice.

Innovative architecture, created during the 19th century to reflect the new age of the bourgeoisie, included the greenhouse of the Botanical Garden constructed by Tilman-Frans Suys in 1826. Built in 1846, the Galeries Royales Saint-Hubert by Jean-Pierre Cluisenaer was the first covered shopping arcade in Europe.

ART NOUVEAU

The influence of the emergent working classes at the end of the 19th century is reflected in the Maison du Peuple (People's House) commis-

Itinerant artist
In 1520, the German painter Albrecht Dürer travelled from Antwerp to Brussels. The diary of his journey is a rich source of information: he recorded which trading routes he took, where he rested and how much he spent along the way.

Opposite: the Magasins Wolfier by Horta
Bottom: the portal of Notre Dame du Sablon

sioned by the trades unions from the architect Victor Horta. Together with Henri van de Velde, Horta is regarded as one of the leading exponents of art nouveau architecture in Belgium. He constructed trend-setting apartment houses and hotels of stone and cast iron. One such building is the house of the cloth merchant Maison Waucquez on Rue des Sables, now the home of the Belgian Comic Strip Centre.

BRUXELLISATION AND FACADISME

In recent times, Brussels has provided architecture with two of its most hideous terms, thanks to a combination of unscrupulous local officials and avaricious 'developers'. **Bruxellisation** refers to the city's willful demolition of treasured buildings and heritage sites. In the 1960s, a period of political laissez-faire led to the razing of architectural landmarks that included masterpieces like Horta's Maison du Peuple. The worst heritage crimes took place in the northern district around the World Trade Centre, Brussels' misguided attempt to ape Manhattan, and in the European District, the site of the European institutions.

Towards the end of the 1980s, citizens were so disheartened by the disastrous examples of new buildings in the city that there was little enthusiasm for contemporary architecture. Instead architects raided the toy box of Flemish vernacular and came up with fake gabled hotels and other uninspired copies. **Facadisme**, the 'art' of gutting and remodelling a building while leaving the facade intact, was the alternative, more enduring legacy. This was the solution the city authorities came up with to satisfy the speculators while appeasing the heritage police. The technique is visible in countless buildings in the city centre: behind many a baroque or Belle Epoque facade lurks a stainless-steel and sheer-glass interior.

There has been a creative backlash after so much desecration. The restored royal district has installed bars and public spaces to attract visitors to the area. Likewise, the Mont des Arts section of the royal and museum district is designed

Place St Gery

to be admired at night: filtered light highlights the architectural features. Throughout the city, enlightened planners have risked architecturally exciting projects, notably the conversion of abandoned industrial buildings, warehouses and covered markets into cultural centres.

Art

When, in 1430, Brussels made the abrupt transition from the rule of the Dukes of Brabant to that of the Dukes of Burgundy, it was not long before art that reflected the new régime's cosmopolitan tastes began to appear, art so significant it influenced the Renaissance artists of Italy.

One of the most renowned masters of Flemish painting, Rogier van der Weyden, settled in Brussels and remained there until his death in 1464. His style was propagated thereafter by other artists including Colijn de Coter. Brussels was also home to many acclaimed wood carvers during this era. A number of their works, the famed Brussels carved altars, were exported to Germany and Sweden. In the 16th century, Barend van Orley was responsible for a renewed heyday of painting in Brussels, introducing the Renaissance to the city. And last but not least, one of Belgium's most famous artists, Pieter Brueghel (1520–69), although born in the village of Brueghel, lived

Below: Descent from the Cross *by Rubens*
Bottom: Brueghel's Dulle Griet

in Brussels for much of his adult life, and died in his house at 123 Rue Haute.

At the same time, Brussels was developing into the centre of European tapestry making, which first became established in the city in the 15th century. Records show that the art of rug weaving was handed down through a number of families throughout the 16th to 18th century. Thus the history of the Brussels Gobelin tapestry trade mirrors the development of Flemish painting. Beginning with the Late Gothic style, so important at the Burgundian court, Flemish art continues through the Renaissance, with its Italian influence, all the way to the baroque style, as evidenced by the ecstatic animation in the paintings of Peter Paul Rubens.

Thereafter, Belgian painting fell into decline until 1816 when Frenchman Jacques-Louis David settled in Brussels.

Below: René Magritte
Bottom: The Sphinx *by Knopf*

BELGIAN SURREALISM

In the late 19th to early 20th century, art once again flourished with the advent of artists such as the Surrealist Paul Delvaux, who was influenced by the most famous visionary of them all, René Magritte. He painted a number of murals for Belgian public buildings; his major paintings include *The Wind and The Song* and *The Human Condition.* An entire room in the Museum of Modern Art is devoted to Magritte's work.

Theatre and Music

Popular foreign opinion to the contrary, Brussels is in fact a vibrant city, blessed with a musical soul, a dynamic arts scene, engaging museums, multicultural aspirations, and some sassy venues. With the new millennium, and its stint as European Capital of Culture in 2000, the city sought to shake off its provincial image and emerge from the shadow of Paris and Amsterdam. Until Brussels 2000, the cultural scene had been characterised by fragmentation instead of a healthy diversity and synergy.

With the wealth of theatres, night clubs and cultural centres in Brussels, there is no shortage of entertainment, and tickets are usually easy to come by. The weekly *Bulletin* magazine gives details of concerts and cultural events; alternatively you can consult their website in advance (www.whatson.be). The Tourist Office in the Grand' Place runs a ticket-booking service (tel: 0800-21 221); their website is www.art-events.be Alternatively, tickets can be obtained from the FNAC bookstore on Rue Neuve, tel: 02 203 2211.

CLASSICAL CONCERTS

The major venue for classical and mainstream concerts is the Palais des Beaux-Arts on Rue Ravenstein – now known, somewhat tackily, as Bozar – (tel: 02 507 8200 or 02 511 3433 for details of their impressive calendar of events). The cream of the crop of Brussels theatres is the National Opera in the Théâtre Royal de la Monnaie (tel: 02 229 1211), which stages operas and ballets and is located on Place de la Monnaie. There are several theatres in the city centre: Théâtre Royal des Galeries in the Galerie du Roi (tel: 02 512 0407), Théâtre National de Belgique on Place Rogier (tel: 02 203 5303), Cirque Royal, Rue de l'Enseignement 81 (tel: 02 218 2015). For Dutch theatre, try Beursschouwburg on Rue Auguste Orts near the Bourse (tel: 02 513 8290), or Vlaamse Schouwburg on Rue de Laeken 146 (tel: 02 217 6937). One special attraction is the

Surrealism lives

Brussels delights in its image as 'capital of surrealism', a reputation it has maintained long after the departure of from the scene of Delvaux and Magritte. Brussels-based François Schuiten, Belgium's most important living comic-strip artist, specialises in retro-futuristic parallel universes, whether in comic-book form, in multimedia, or for artworks that grace city Metro stations.

Theatre poster

renowned Toone VII Marionette Theatre, Petite Rue des Bouchers 21, tel: 02 511 7137) near the Town Hall. It has been performing folklore pieces since 1830 which can usually be understood even by those with no knowledge of the language.

ENGLISH-LANGUAGE THEATRE

There is an active English-language theatre scene which stages high-quality performances of English, Irish and American works. Check *The Bulletin* for details.

CONTEMPORARY MUSIC

Fans of contemporary music should check out Ancienne Belgique, Forest-National and Le Botanique. Jazz lovers are well catered for in Brussels: L'Archiduc, New York Café Jazz Club, Sounds and Travers are all popular venues, offering a range of styles.

Travers, the city's main jazz venue, is one of the settings for the Brussels Jazz Marathon. In the course of one weekend in May, the sounds of mellow jazz, Dixieland, blues and the cutting-edge of acid jazz echo around the cool clubs of the St-Boniface, Avenue Louise and St-Géry districts. Although such luminaries as Toots Thielemans, Belgium's legendary jazz musician, regularly appear here, Le Travers is best known for its jamming sessions and warm welcome.

Brussels has an excellent ballet company

Festivals

As befits the Capital of Europe, Brussels satisfies its cosmopolitan audiences with world-class events, particularly festivals of classical music. However, the city also keeps in touch with its medieval heritage by celebrating heartfelt folkloric displays of Brueghelian excess.

For music lovers, things get going in March with **Ars Musica**, a frenetic 2-week festival of contemporary classical music. The public has the opportunity to attend rehearsals, master classes, musical talks and concerts. In May, the prestigious

Kunsten Arts Festival focuses on the performing arts, notably ballet, contemporary dance, theatre and opera. In the same month, the week-long **Baroque Spring Festival**, a musical extravaganza devoted to chamber music, takes place on Place du Grand-Sablon. The last weekend of the month is a treat for jazz lovers, with the **Brussels Jazz Marathon** culminating in a series of concerts on the Grand' Place.

In summer, some of the best folklore festivals are staged. In early July the colourful, medieval pageant called the **Ommegang** comes to town. The procession, which began as a lavish display by the burghers of Brussels gained a new lease of life as a tribute to Charles V in 1539, the ruler who declared Brussels the capital of his boundless empire. Today, a parade of costumed cavaliers, and Burgundian lords and ladies wends its way from the Sablon to the Grand' Place and culminates in a massive evening spectacle on the square. Equally authentic is the **Meyboom**, staged in early August, a recreation of a medieval ceremony recalling the successful defence of the city against Leuven in 1213. Another engaging event is the biennial Carpet of Flowers, when the Grand' Place is 'carpeted' by 700,000 begonias forming an impressive, if garish, patchwork of scenes from Belgian folklore. There is a sound and light display and fireworks on the opening night.

Below: a busker in Brussels
Bottom: dancing at a local festival

FOOD AND DRINK

Brussels' Specialities

Brussels prides itself on a number of culinary specialities, including the following well-known dishes: *chicons au gratin* (chicory rolled in ham in a Béchamel sauce); *anguilles au vert* (river eel with herb sauce); *choesels au Madère* (sweet breads with Madeira sauce and champignons); Flemish *carbonade* (beef stewed in beer); Brussels sprouts (boiled then tossed in butter); Brussels-style mussels, which are usually eaten with French fries, and *stoemp* (a hotpot of potatoes and vegetables served with sausage).

From the area around Brussels and just as highly recommended are: *Mechelen* asparagus (in a sauce of hard-boiled eggs, chopped parsley and melted butter, a real delicacy); chicken or fish *waterzooï* (a delicate creamy stew-cum-soup); jugged hare Flemish style (prepared with onions and served with stewed prunes).

Anyone who thinks French fries are an invention of the fast food industry is mistaken. Although they have only gained such enormous popularity in recent times, they were actually invented about 300 years ago in Liège and the surrounding area. They are available not only at snack stands on street corners but also as an accompaniment to a fine meal in the best gourmet temples, and they are usually very good.

In addition to the wide variety of Belgian baked goods, the specialities of Brussels include: sugar cakes, *pain cramique* (raisin bread), *spekuloos* biscuits (spicy biscuits), *pain d'amandes* (almond bread); and Brussels waffles *(gaufres)*.

Perhaps most importantly, Brussels is known as the world capital of pralines and chocolates. Leonidas are the most common and cheapest brand, but they still taste good; more expensive, and utterly delicious, are Neuhaus, Godiva and Wittamer.

BELGIAN BEER

The national drink of Belgium is beer, brewed throughout the country in about 115 breweries. There are more than 400 different kinds of beers and 200 different flavour variations. The beers of Brussels are renowned for the natural fermentation process as, for instance, in *Faro* beer, a wheat beer brewed according to an ancient recipe. Also noteworthy is *Gueuze-Lambic*, brewed from a mixture of half barley and half wheat. With a shot of cherry juice added, it is known as *Kriek-Lambic*, and should definitely be sampled. A closer look at the brewing process can be had at the Belgian Brewers' Museum on the Grand' Place *(see page 18)* and at the Gueuze Museum on Rue Gheude.

RESTAURANTS FOR GOURMETS

The Belgian capital has more than 1,800 restaurants. The tourist office in Brussels *(see page 97)* publishes a

---

Good tastes

The Place Ste-Catherine and Fish Market area is justly famed for seafood restaurants that have an informal atmosphere and high-quality food. The area around the Grand' Place, and especially Rue des Bouchers, is full of small eateries, cheaper restaurants that also serve memorable food, and although many places are devoted to tourists the quality is generally high. Stand-bys are traditional favourites like mussels with frites, steak and *waterzooï*.

brochure annually with the title *Gourmet*, featuring the most important establishments along with opening times and prices. The selection belows includes just a few of the best-known restaurants in Brussels, but you'll find that you can eat well at almost any neighbourhood tavern.

€€€ = Expensive (over €100 for two); **€€** = Moderate (€50–100 for two); **€** = Inexpensive (under €50 for two).

Comme Chez Soi, 23 Place Rouppe, tel: 02 512 2921. Generally regarded as the best restaurant in Belgium, sporting three Michelin stars. Owner and chef Pierre Wijnants has transformed Belgian cuisine by bringing traditional ingredients like beer and hopshoots back onto the gourmet menu. The small, Art Nouveau-style restaurant is often booked weeks ahead. **€€€**

Bruneau, 73–75 Avenue Broustin, tel: 02 427 6978. Chef Jean-Pierre Bruneau, a master of nouvelle cuisine, serves exquisite dishes inspired by the seasons in his rather pompous and heavily decorated – but three-Michelin starred – restaurant in the Ganshoren district. **€€€**

Mussels in Brussels

La Maison du Cygne, 1 Grand' Place, tel: 02 511 8244. Elegant and romantic French restaurant with an exceptional wine cellar. While diners overdose on truffles and *foie gras*, they can enjoy superb views over the historic square. **€€€**

L'Alban Chambon, in the Hôtel Métropole, 31 Place de Brouckère, tel: 02 217 2300. Serves French-inspired cuisine in plush surroundings. Specialities include perfect potatoes with langoustines, and truffles and scallops with a delicious truffle vinaigrette. The wine list and cheese selection are excellent. **€€€**

L'Ecailler du Palais Royal, 18 Rue Bodenbroek, tel: 02 512 8751. Book well ahead for this exclusive and formal food haven in the Sablon district, that serves some of the best fish and seafood specialities in town. **€€€**

La Villa Romaine, 75 Avenue du Vivier d'Oie, tel: 02 374 3163. In the Bois de la Cambre is the romantic set in an airy conservatory. Specialities include oysters in champagne, duck with figs and chocolate soufflé. **€€€**

De l'Ogenblik, 1 Galerie des Princes, tel: 02 511 6151. Offers fine food served by friendly staff in a popular and elegant Parisian-style bistro setting on the edge of the Galeries Royales Saint-Hubert. **€€–€€€**

La Belle Maraîchère, 11 Place Ste-Catherine, tel: 02 512 9759. Of the many fish restaurants in Brussels' old harbour, this is one of the best and most famous, for its rustic décor and seafood specialities like the *waterzooï de trois poissons*. €€–€€€

La Porte des Indes, 455 Avenue Louise, tel: 02 647 8651. Superb Indian food – probably the best in Brussels – discreetly served by waiters wearing traditional dress in an old house decorated with Indian antiques. €€–€€€

La Quincaillerie, 45 Rue du Page, tel: 02 533 9833. If you fancy dinner in unusual surroundings, try a trendy converted hardware store. It's perhaps a little too aware of its own modish good looks, but it's perennially popular, not least for its fine seafood dishes. €€–€€€

La Truite d'Argent, 23 Quai au Bois à Brûler, tel: 02 219 9546. Attractive 19th-century interior, plus a terrace on Place Ste-Catherine. Owner Michel Smeesters relishes the history and traditions of the place, and his beautifully presented fish and lobster specialities are highly recommended. €€–€€€

Aux Armes de Bruxelles, 13 Rue des Bouchers, tel: 02 511 5550. In the heart of the Ilot Sacré restaurant district, this is one of the city's best establishments, well respected for its high-quality Belgian cuisine at reasonable prices. €€

Brasserie de la Roue d'Or, 26 Rue des Chapeliers, tel: 02 514 2554. The brasserie décor is a mixture of mirrored Art Nouveau and homage to René Magritte. Service and atmosphere are familiar and friendly and the Belgian food is great. €€

La Grande Porte, 9 Rue Notre Seigneur, tel: 02 512 8998. A real gem, tucked away in a side street off the Sablon. It's a small bistro with eccentric décor serving traditional Belgian cuisine. You can dine outside when the weather permits. €€

In 't Spinnekopke, 1 Place du Jardin-aux-Fleurs, tel: 02 511 8695. One of Brussels' oldest restaurants specialises in dishes using Belgian beer, and also does good work with mussels. €€

Kasbah, 20 Rue Antoine Dansaert, tel: 02 502 4026. An authentic taste of Morocco on a hip street in down-town Brussels; serving generous portions in dimly lit surroundings. €€

La Manufacture, 12 Rue Notre-Dame du Sommeil, tel: 02 502 2525. Large restaurant housed in a converted factory. The décor is ultra-modern and the food is popular with a trendy crowd. Garden open in summer. €€

Le Marmiton, 43A Rue des Bouchers, tel: 02 511 7910. Trencherman quantity combines with quality at a reasonable price. If all Ilot restaurants maintained the high standards of Le Marmiton, there would be no need for warning visitors to the area to be on their guard against sharp operators. €€

Pablo's, 51 Rue de Namur, tel: 02 502 4135. Situated between Porte de Namur and Place Royale, this relaxed restaurant serves great margaritas and solid, spicy Tex-Mex food. €€

Le Rocher Fleuri, 19 Rue Franklin, tel: 02 735 0021. In the European quarter, this Vietnamese restaurant serves a delicious all-you-can-eat buffet at lunchtime and evenings. €€

Vincent, 8–10 Rue des Dominicains, tel: 02 511 2303. You walk past the kitchens to reach the unusual, maritime-themed dining room here. The traditional Brussels fare – mussels, steaks and others standbys – is good value for money. €€

Au Stekerlapatte, 4 Rue des Prêtres, tel: 02 512 8681. Delightful and very popular restaurant with a jovial atmosphere and a long list of Belgian specialities, including *stoemp* with steak tartare, rabbit stewed in beer, and

Brussels chicken served with mushrooms. €–€€

Chez Léon, 18 Rue des Bouchers, tel: 02 511 1415. A Brussels institution since 1893 that serves up thousands of mussels in various tasty guises every day. The quality is always reliable, and the service is fast but friendly. Try to get a table in the more atmospheric ground floor. €–€€

King Hwa, 240 Chaussee de Louvain, tel: 02 230 1579. Excellent Chinese restaurant located out of the city centre in Saint-Josse, with a huge menu covering all regions of China. Great value for money. €–€€

Paradiso, 34 Rue Duquesnoy, tel: 02 512 5232. A warm welcome, and pasta and pizza just like mamma used to make, in a hidden gem not far from the Grand' Place. €–€€

Passage To India, 223 Chaussée de Louvain, tel: 02 735 3147. Unpretentious Indian restaurant, which has earned a following for its reliable food. €–€€

A Malte, 30 Rue Berckmans, tel: 02 539 1015. A café with a relaxed, bohemian atmosphere where you could, in theory, hang around all day, starting with breakfast in the garden followed by lunch, tea and dinner. Good-value brasserie food. €

L'Achepot, 1 Place Ste-Catherine, tel: 02 511 6211. Popular and casual restaurant with a terrace, serving traditional Belgian specialities, including some far from awful offal dishes. €

La Bonne Humeur, 244 Chaussée de Louvain, tel: 02 230 7169. This inexpensive neighbourhood restaurant serves inexpensive mussels and fries. Go early, since there are often queues and the kitchen closes at 9.30pm. €

't Kelderke, 15 Grand' Place, tel: 02 513 7344. Plain, hearty Belgian fare such as *stoemp*, *carbonnades* and *moules*, served until 2am in a convivial, low-ceilinged cellar with the kitchen in plain view, and the Grand' Place outside the front door for an after-dinner stroll. €

La Mirabelle, 49 Chaussée de Boondael, tel: 02 649 5173. One of the good-value brasseries in the lively area surrounding Université Libre de Bruxelles, frequented by students. A large garden is open in summer. €

The Lunch Company, 16 Rue de Namur, tel: 02 502 0976. Conveniently located in a narrow street between Place Royale and the shops in the Upper City, this is a quiet restaurant serving light lunches and excellent afternoon tea, coffee and cakes. €

Het Warm Water, 19 Rue des Renards, tel: 02 513 9159. Just off the Place du jeu de Balle, this delightful place serves great breakfasts, lunches, brunches and snacks. Good beer plus children's room. No reservations or credit cards. €

CAFÉS AND BARS

The Flemish claim that in Belgium there is a bar or café on every street corner, but Brussels seems to be even better served than that. The capital may at first appear a rather dull city of bureaucrats, but if you explore the city's many outlets, from small corner bars to the trendy venues or the traditional smoky brown cafés, you will soon discover that both the city and its inhabitants are quite definitely alive. Begin the evening at one of the many *café-terraces*, but don't bother going to the more fashionable bars before midnight; you will find only other tourists. A few *café-terraces* are heated in winter, but most will only appear with the first sunshine: like Parisians, the people of Brussels enjoy watching the crowds from a seat on the pavement.

Near the Bourse is a Brussels institution, **Le Falstaff** (19–25 Rue Henri

Maus, tel: 02 511 9877), an extremely busy and grand art deco café where everyone seems to end up either for an aperitif, afternoon snack or on the weekends, when they are open till 5am, for an early morning coffee. The terrace or the lovely lounge of the **Métropole Hotel** on Place de Brouckère are popular places for an early-evening, typically Brussels aperitif of *half-en-half*, half white wine, half sparkling wine. **Le Corbeau** on Rue Saint-Michel (just off Rue Neuve) is a friendly place for a good and inexpensive lunch, and comes alive at night. Here you can amuse your friends by trying to drink a yard of ale from a *chevalier* (a large glass on a wooden frame). Traditional 'brown' bars in this area are **La Bécasse** (beer-tasting on request) on Rue de Tabora and **Au Bon Vieux Temps** on Rue du Marché-aux-Herbes.

The wood-panelled Art Deco bar **L'Espérance** (1–3 Rue de Finistère, tel: 02 217 3247) is a regular 'brown café' during the day, but turns into a funky bar at night. **A La Mort Subite** (7 Rue Montagne-aux-Herbes Potagères, tel: 02 512 8664) was the favourite hang out of the great Belgian

Streetside tables at one of Brussels' many cafés

singer Jacques Brel, and it sells a range of snacks and beers, including its own 'Mort Subite' or 'Sudden Death'. A favourite watering hole for the Flemish speaking 'in' crowd is the **L'Archiduc** (6 Rue Antoine Dansaert, tel: 02 512 0652), which has a good selection of Belgian beers and plays live jazz on Sunday afternoons. A similar clientele frequents the nearby **Beursschouwburg** at 22 Rue Auguste Orts. Its unappealing exterior opens into a stylish and spacious bar.

The bars along Rue du Marché-au-Charbon and Place St-Gery are buzzing with life on weekend nights, while the Place du Sablon is more popular with the slightly more *chichi* French-speaking community.

TEAROOMS

A favourite afternoon passtime for Belgians is to visit a patisserie or tea room for a cup of coffee and a *gaufre* (waffle), a pancake or a pastry. The excellent chain of restaurants **Le Pain Quotidien** serve delicious breakfasts, lunches and home-made bread and cakes, which are eaten around one large table. One of the city's finest patisseries is **Wittamer** (12–13 Place du Grand-Sablon), which sells a mouth-watering selection of hand-made chocolates and gâteaux.

NIGHTLIFE

Cabaret and nightclubs

As the theatres empty after the last performance, the Brussels late-night scene comes to life. Cartagena is a lively salsa bar and disco; Bazaar, Fool Moon and Tour & Taxis are fashionable clubs. Le Sparrow and Mirano Continental are fairly smart well established discos. If all this activity sharpens your appetite, there are around 50 downtown restaurants which stay open into the small hours. Among the best are Falstaff, Cap, La Grande Porte and Ateliers de la Grande-Ile.

The daily newspapers contain information about entertainment in Brussels. Visitors can reserve tickets for the opera, concerts and theatre productions at the Brussels Tourist International at the Grand' Place.

In Brussels there are theatres that perform dramatic works in both French and Dutch. There is a lively English-language theatre scene, with groups specialising in pre-Shakespeare, Irish and American drama and comedy. Check *The Bulletin* for details of events.

Chocolate – in many guises – is one of the best buys

Most of the important concerts take place in the Palais de Beaux-Arts (now known, less formally and less elegantly, as Bozar). Opera and ballet productions are performed at the Théâtre Royale de la Monnaie (the National Opera House), the most famous stage in Brussels. Aside from these large venues, there is a host of smaller theatres that stage less mainstream productions.

Over 50 dance companies work in the Brussels region, some of which are leading names in the world of contemporary dance. Among these are the troupes of Anna Teresa De Keersmaeker and Wim Vandekeybus.

Some foreign-language films in Brussels are dubbed, but most of them are also shown in the original language, with Dutch and French subtitles. There are several major cinemas in the city centre, many of them multiplexes. Kinepolis has 26 screens including an IMAX screen. Nova (3 Rue d'Arenberg) is an arthouse cinema, and Musée du Cinema (9 Rue Baron Horta) has two projection rooms that show classic films from the pre-war era, with silent films accompanied by a pianist.

SHOPPING

A shopping spree in Brussels is usually a pleasure, since the wide array of shops, markets and shopping centres offers something for everybody. The city is justifiably famous for its diamonds, lace and fine hand-made chocolates, although those in search of the latest fashions will also be satisfied. The upmarket international fashion designers such as Gucci, Versace and Nina Ricci have shops around Place Stéphanie, Avenue Louise and Boulevard de Waterloo. In this area there are also a cluster of prestigious, upmarket modern shopping galleries: Galerie Espace Louise and Galerie Louise at Place Louise; and Galerie de la Toison d'Or and Galerie d'Ixelles at Porte de Namur.

For the trendiest names among Belgian designers, including Olivier Strelli, head for Rue Antoine Dansaert, where De Stijl and other shops sell cutting edge fashion. The elegant 19th-century Galeries Royales Saint-Hubert are home to several upmarket design shops and excellent bookshops and gift shops.

Casual wear and high-street fashion are found in many outlets along the main shopping street, rue Neuve, while the galeries off the main drag offer more esoteric wares. Lovers of antiques should check out the shops around Place du Grand-Sablon. For second-hand books, try the bookshops in Galerie Bortier on Rue du Marché-aux-Herbes. Comic strip fans can go mad in the shop of the Belgian Comic Strip Centre (20 Rue des Sables), Le Depot (108 Rue du Midi), both for new and second hand comic strips, or La Boutique Tintin on Rue de la Colline. De Bier Tempel on Rue du Marché-aux-Herbes sells all kinds of things relating to Belgian beer, including home-brewing kits for the real enthusiast; try the Brussels Corner next door for above-average souvenirs. Designer-milliner Elvis Pompilio displays his startling collection of hats on Rue du Lombard. Madonna is said to be one of his clients.

MARKETS

Markets offer a glimpse of real Brussels and a good way to spend a weekend morning. The tourist office provides an information leaflet on all markets.

Antiques Market, place du Grand Sablon, Saturday 9am–6pm, Sunday 9am–2pm. Good quality silverware, pottery, paintings and jewellery.

Art Market, Parvis Saint-Pierre, Uccle, Sunday 10am–1pm.

Flea Market, Place du Jeu de Balle, daily 7am–2pm, but best and most atmospheric on Sunday morning.

Flower Market, Grand' Place, Tuesday to Sunday 8am–6pm.

Food and Textile Market, Marché du Midi, near the South Station, Sunday 7am–2pm. A large and colourful market – great fun and the place to buy cheap herbs and spices, all kinds of food and pot plants.

Non-residents of the European Union are able to purchase certain items without paying value-added tax (TVA) – or more accurately to be able to claim it back.

> ### What to buy
> Brussels is known for its fine beer, chocolate, crystalware, diamonds and lace. You'll find shops selling these and other souvenirs around the Grand' Place, by Manneken-Pis, and near the Bourse and the Théâtre Royal de la Monnaie.

PRACTICAL INFORMATION

Getting There

BY PLANE

Brussels National Airport, at Zaventem, is 14km (8 miles) northeast of Brussels. The following airlines all fly to Brussels from the UK: British Airways (UK, tel: 0870 850 9850; Belgium, tel: 02 717 3217; www.britishairways.com); BMi (UK, tel: 0870 607 0555; Belgium, tel: 02 713 1824; www.flybmi.com); Virgin Express (UK, tel 0870 730 1134; Belgium, tel: 070 353637; www.virgin-express.com); and Belgian carrier SN Brussels Airlines (UK, tel: 020 7559 9787; Belgium, tel: 02 754 1900; www.flysn.com). Three trains an hour connect the airport with Brussels' Gare du Nord, Gare Centrale and Gare du Midi railway stations. A taxi to Gare Centrale costs about €35.

BY SEA

Zeebrugge is served once daily by car ferry from Hull by P&O Ferries (UK. tel: 08705 202020; Belgium, tel: 02 710 6444; www.poferries.com); and once every two days from Rosyth (Edinburgh) by Superfast Ferries (UK, tel: 0870 234 0870; Belgium, tel: 050 252292; www.superfast.com). Trains from Zeebrugge to Brussels depart every hour during the day. You can also sail to Calais and Dunkirk and drive from there to Brussels in about two hours.

BY TRAIN

There are regular international services from Paris, Amsterdam, Cologne and Zeebrugge, the latter connecting with car-ferry services from Britain. The direct rail service from London to Brussels is operated by Eurostar (tel: 08701 606600 from within the UK; www.eurostar.co.uk). The journey time is 2 hours and 40 minutes. The Eurostar number in Brussels is 02 528 2828.

Travel time from Brussels is 20 minutes to Leuven or Mechelen, 30 minutes to Antwerp or Ghent, 50 minutes to Namur, 60 minutes to Tournai, 65 minutes to Liège and 75 minutes to Ostend.

Some special offers:

Half-fare privilege ticket: this affords a 50 percent discount for a period of one month throughout the entire railway network.

Senior citizens discount: senior citizens holding a Rail-Europ Senior Ticket receive 50 percent discount on rail travel throughout Belgium.

B-Tourrail: Those wishing to make excursions from Brussels into the outlying areas should consider purchasing the tourist ticket B-Tourrail. It is valid throughout the entire railway network for five days within a period of a month. The ticket is issued either for first- or second-class travel. Children under six travel free while older children and young people receive discounts.

B-Excurions: all-in tickets include reduced rail fares, entrance fees and bus or tram fares.

Weekend Return: 40 percent reduced tickets if the outward journey is made on Friday, Saturday or Sunday and the return journey is on Saturday, Sunday or Monday. Small groups receive a 60 percent reduction.

Go Pass: Issued for under 26 year olds, allowing 10 2nd class journeys between any 2 stations in Belgium.

Additionally, it is possible to book day trips with or without supplementary bus excursions. Information about these offers can be obtained at larger railway stations (tel: 02 528 2828; www.sncb.be).

BY CAR

Brussels, one of Western Europe's traffic hubs, has a superb motorway network. The E19 comes in from Paris 310km (193 miles) to the southeast and, via Antwerp, from Amsterdam 232km (144 miles) to the north; the E40 comes in via Ghent from Ostend and Zeebrugge 114km (71 miles) to the west and, via Liège and Leuven, from Cologne 228km (142 miles) to the east; the E411 arrives, via Namur, from Luxembourg 220km (137 miles) to the southeast. All motorways converge on the motorway ring about 10km (6 miles) outside the city centre. The fastest means of getting from the UK to Belgium by car is with Eurotunnel (tel: 0990 353535; www.eurotunnel.com) from

Folkestone to Calais. In summer there are up to four trains every hour.

A driver's licence, vehicle registration papers, warning triangle and a nationality sticker on the rear of the vehicle are necessary when entering Belgium. The speed limit is 50km/h (31mph) within a town and 120km/h (70mph) on the motorway or 4-lane highways. On all other roads it is 90km/h (55mph). In Belgium *priorité à droite* (right-of-way for those on the right) is usually valid, unless the road you are on is marked with an orange diamond-shaped sign, in which case you have priority over those coming from

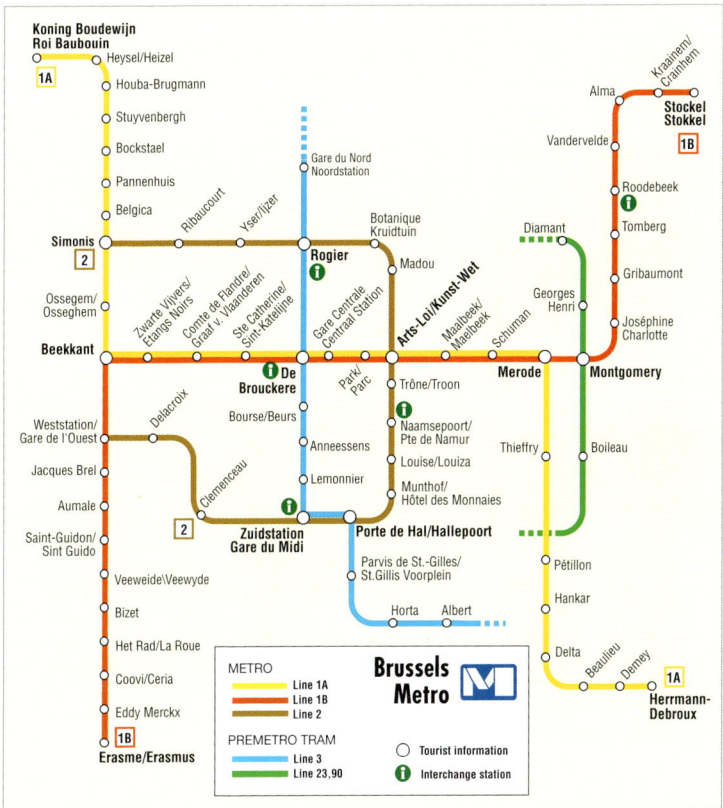

Brussels Metro

METRO
Line 1A
Line 1B
Line 2

PREMETRO TRAM
Line 3
Line 23, 90

○ Tourist information
ⓘ Interchange station

the right. It is illegal for children under the age of 12 to sit in the front passenger seat if there is room in the back seat.

Emergencies: in case of an accident with personal injury, call the **emergency number 100** to request help. This number is valid throughout the country. Brussels emergency service: RACB, tel: 078 152 000. TCB, tel: 233 2211/070 344 777.

Automobile clubs: Royal Automobil Club de Belgique (RACB), 53 Rue d'Arlon/Aarlenstraat, 1040 Brussels, tel: 02 287 0900; Touring Club Royal de Belgique (TCB), 44 Rue de la Loi/Wetstraat, 1040 Brussels, tel: 02 233 2211.

Getting Around

PARKING

Parking in the centre of Brussels is becoming increasingly difficult due to the volume of traffic. There are parking meters, but it's probably easier to use the multi-storey carparks. Be sure to take note of the closing times.

CITY RAILWAY

Belgian trains are run by the SNCB (Sociéte Nationale des Chemins Fers

The clean and efficient tram system is a good way to get around

Belges), metro, buses and trams by the STIB (Société des Transports Intercommunaux de Bruxelles), and buses to outlying areas by tec and De Lijn. All stations and most tram and bus stops have transit maps.

Among the stations and stops of the sncb, those most important for the tourist are the ones of the north–south underground line (Pré-Metro and tram lines 51, 55, 58, 81 and 90). These run through the city centre between North Station (Gare du Nord) and South Station (Gare du Midi). The most important stops are Congrès, Central Station (Gare Centrale) and Chapelle. Note that a transfer is possible, at Place de Brouckère, to the Metro lines 1a-b and at Place Rogier to Metro line 2. The sncb also serves Greater Brussels with about 20 suburban stations.

UNDERGROUND (METRO)

The Brussels underground network is quick, clean and efficient and consists of two underground lines (with a length of about 33km/20 miles) which connect the eastern and western parts of the city. The underground network is supplemented by three Pré-Metro lines. Pré-Metro means that the underground tracks are also used by the trams, which, somewhat confusingly, operate both above and under ground.

The underground lines

Metro 1a: This line runs west of the city centre in a north–south direction before crossing through the city centre and the Quartier Léopold in an east–west direction. The stations are: Heysel (Atomium), Houba-Brugman, Stuyvenbergh, Bockstael (near Parc de Laeken), Pannenhuis, Belgica, Simonis, Osseghem, Beekkant, Etangs Noirs, Comte de Flandre, Ste Catherine, de Brouckère (interchange with Pré Metro), Gare Centrale, Parc, Arts-Loi, Maelbeek, Schuman, Mérode, Thieffry, Petillon, Hankar, Delta, Beaulieu, Demey, Hermann Debroux.

Metro 1b: This line runs west of the city centre before crossing through the city and the Quartier Léopold in an east–west direction. The stations are: Bizet, Veeweyde, St Guido, Aumale, Jacques Brel, Gare de l'Ouest, Beekkant. Here it joins the line 1a until Mérode. At that station, the Metro 1b branches to the northeast, stopping at the following stations: Montgomery, Josephine Charlotte, Gribaumont, Tomberg, Roodebeek, Vandervelde, Alma, Kraainem, Stokkel.

Metro line 2 (Trams 2, 18, 19, 32, 101, 103): This follows the course of the boulevard ring along its northeastern and eastern sectors, with the following stations: Simonis, Ribaucourt, Yser, Rogier, Botanique, Madou, Arts-Loi (transfer station with Metro 1a–b), Trône, Porte de Namur, Louise, Hotel des Monnaies, Porte de Hal, Zuidstation and Clémenceau.

Pré-Metro line 3 (Trams 52, 55, 58, 81 and 90): This north–south line crosses through the city centre following the large boulevards. The stations are: Gare du Nord, Rogier (interchange with line 2), de Brouckère (interchange with Metro 1a–b),

Bourse, Anneessens, Lemonnier, Gare du Midi.

Pré-Metro line 5 (Trams 23 and 90): This north–south line runs east of the city centre along the 'middle' ring road, linking the boroughs of Schaerbeek and Etterbeek. The stations are: Bd A Reyers, Diamant, Georges Henri, Montgomery (interchange with the Metro 1b), Boileau.

Art in the Metro

Contemporary Belgian artists have transformed the underground stations into veritable galleries of art with specially commissioned paintings. The TIB *(see page 97)* and the Information Office of the STIB have a free brochure about art in the Metro. Special conducted tours are also available. For more information, contact the tourist office.

BUS

The STIB has about 30 bus and tram lines (two-digit numbers) covering the city. The tec and De Lijn buses, which operate about 70 bus lines, carry a three-digit number plus one or two letters. They serve the suburbs and outlying areas and depart mainly from the North Station and the South Station.

TICKETS

The STIB tourist ticket is good for unlimited travel within a 24-hour period. It can be purchased at the reception of the TIB (Brussels Tourist Office), the Town Hall, Grand' Place, at the Metro information offices or at the railway stations.

Single tickets are available as well as tickets for five or 10 trips. They can be purchased from the driver, at the ticket windows and automatic ticket machines in the Metro stations and in some stationery shops. Tickets must be inserted into the electronic cancelling machines before boarding. These are found at the entrances to underground stations as well as at the bus stops. A transfer between tram, Metro or bus is free within a one-hour period. Children under 12 ride free on the STIB transit network.

Red and white or blue and white signs mark the tram and bus stops. The underground stations are marked by a large white M on a blue background.

CITY TOURS

In summer months, some travel agencies offer conducted tours of the city by coach, bike, boat or on foot. Enquire at the tourist office on the Grand' Place (tel: 02 513 8940).

Facts for the Visitor

VISAS

Citizens of the European Union do not need a passport or visa but they must have an ID card. Citizens of most other European countries, the USA, Australia, Canada, Japan and some other countries can enter Belgium without a visa. If in doubt, check with the Belgian consulate in your country of origin, or with your travel agent.

CUSTOMS

Non-EU members can bring 400 cigarettes, one bottle of spirits, two of wine and 50g of perfume; EU citizens can import unlimited quantities of liquor and tobacco from other EU member states, provided they can prove it is for their own personal use.

CURRENCY REGULATIONS

There is neither a limit nor a declaration requirement for travellers' cheques or foreign currency.

INFORMATION

In the UK: Belgian Tourist Office (Brussels and Wallonia), 217 Marsh Wall, London E14 9FJ, tel: 020 7531 0390; fax: 020 7531 0393; e-mail: info@belgiumtheplaceto.be; www.belgiumtheplaceto.be. Belgian Tourist Office (Brussels and Flanders), 1A Cavendish Square, London W1G 0LD, tel: 020 7307 7730; fax: 020 7307 7731; e-mail: info@visitflanders.co.uk; www.visitflanders.co.uk.

In the US: 780 Third Ave, Suite 1501, New York, NY 10017, tel: (212) 758 8130; fax: (212) 355 7675; e-mail: info@visitbelgium.com; www.visitbelgium.com.

In Canada: PO Box 760, Succursal NDG, Montreal, Quebec H4A 3S2, tel: (514) 457 2888; fax: (514) 457 9447; e-mail: info@visitbelgium.com; www.visitbelgium.com.

In Belgium: Brussels International Tourism, Hôtel de Ville (Town Hall), Grand-Place, tel: 02 513 8940; fax: 02 514 4538; e-mail: info@brusselstourism.be; www.brusselsdiscovery.com. Belgian Tourist Office, 63 Rue du Marché-aux-Herbes, 1000 Brussels, tel: 02 504 0390; fax: 02 504 0270; www.opt.be; www.visitflanders.com.

CURRENCY AND EXCHANGE

Belgium's currency is the euro (€), comprised of 100 cents. There are six euro banknotes: 5, 10, 20, 50, 100 and 500 euros; and eight euro coins: 1 cent, 2 cents, 5 cents, 10 cents, 20 cents and 50 cents, and 1 and 2 euros. Currency can be exchanged in all banks during opening hours (generally Monday–Friday 9am–noon and 2–4pm). The bureaux de change in the following stations are open daily: Gare du Nord: 7am–9.30pm; Gare Centrale: 7am–9pm; Gare du Midi: 6.45am–10pm. The main international credit cards (Mastercard, Visa, American Express) are widely accepted.

OPENING TIMES

Shops are normally open Monday to Saturday from 9am–6pm, although some of them close on Monday. There are a few late-night shops downtown, and the neighbourhood 'corner store' may be open until 9pm. On Friday larger stores and supermarkets stay open until 9pm. Bakeries and patisseries also open on Sunday mornings. The majority of museums open on Sunday, but may close on Mondays. The name and address of the closest pharmacist on duty and open is indicated at every pharmacy.

PUBLIC HOLIDAYS

Aside from the main religious holidays and 1 May (Labour Day), Belgium celebrates its national holiday on 21 July, Assumption of the Virgin on 15 August, All Saints' Day on 1 November and Armistice Day on 11 November. If one of these celebrations falls on a Sunday, the following day is a bank holiday. Apart from tourist shops in the city centre, the vast majority of stores and businesses are closed on public holidays.

POST

Post offices are normally open Monday to Friday from 9am–5pm. Some offices are open on Friday evening and Saturday morning. The post office at

The elegant Galeries Royales Saint-Hubert

Gare du Midi (Avenue Fonsny) is open 24 hours.

TELEPHONE

The telephone rates are posted in the telephone booths; some phones take coins, but most take the telecard (with 20 units), which can be obtained at any post office, newsagents and kiosks.

To make an international call, dial 00 followed by the code of the country: Australia 61; Ireland 353; United Kingdom 44; US and Canada 1.

The country code for Belgium is 32; the city code for Brussels is 02. Even when dialling within Brussels, you still must use the city code – you always dial the area code in Belgium.

TIME

Belgium is six hours ahead of US Eastern Standard Time and one hour ahead of Greenwich Mean Time.

CLIMATE

Most of Belgium has a temperate climate with relatively cool summers and mild winters, although the Ardennes is influenced by the continental conditions. Here, there is about 1,000mm (39ins) of rain fall as opposed to about 800mm (31ins) in Brussels. In summer, be prepared for all weathers:take your sunglasses and an umbrella!

VOLTAGE

The voltage is 220 volts AC; plugs have 2 round pins.

MEDICAL

Visitors from the EU have the right to claim health services which are available to Belgians. UK visitors should obtain Form E111 from the Department of Health prior to departure. Non-EU citizens should definitely have a travellers' health insurance policy. Information can be obtained at travel agencies or private insurance companies.

Standby doctors: available 24 hours a day, tel: 02 479 1818 (French) or 02 242 4344 (Flemish).
Standby dentists: Monday to Saturday 9pm–7am and Saturday 7am to Monday 7am, tel: 02 426 1026 or 02 428 5888.
Anti-Poison Centre: 070 245 245.

EMERGENCIES

Emergency, ambulance and fire brigade, tel: 100.
Police, tel: 101.
Police station: Rue du Marché-au-Charbon, tel: 02 517 9611.

A boat trip along the attractive waterways

Red Cross, tel: 105.
In phone booths: Reverse charge calls from Belgium to UK: 0800 10044; Belgian operator: 1224.

LOST PROPERTY OFFICES

Airport: to recover lost luggage tel: 02 723 6011; property lost on aircraft tel: 02 723 3929; belongings lost at the airport: tel: 02 753 6820.
Train: tel: 02 555 2525.
Metro, bus or tram: tel: 02 515 2394. or enquire at STIB, Avenue de la Toison d'Or 15. If you lose something in the street, try the local police station.

FOREIGNERS IN NEED

Bruxelles Accueil (in several languages), tel: 02 511 8178.
SOS Youth, tel: 02 512 9020, day and night.

DIPLOMATIC MISSIONS

UK, 85 Rue d'Arlon, tel: 02 287 6211.
US, 25–27 Boulevard du Régent, tel: 02 508 2111.
Canada, 2 Avenue de Tervuren, tel: 02 741 0611.
Australia, 6–8 Rue Guimard, tel: 02 286 0500.
Ireland, 189 Rue Froissart, tel: 02 230 5337.
New Zealand, 1 Square de Meeûs, tel: 02 510 1240.

ACCOMMODATION

The Tourist Reservation Office of Brussels International Tourism in the Town Hall at the Grand' Place provides a free list of hotels. The service can be contacted on tel: 02 513 8940; fax: 02 513 8320; e-mail: tourism@ brusselsinternational.be. The Belgian Tourist Reservations service will also book accommodation for you: tel: 02 513 7484; fax: 02 513 9277; e-mail: btr@ hoseca.be. Most hotels in town are business-orientated and offer generous discounts in summer and during weekends. A list of the hotels offering off-peak reductions is also available from the tourist office. This makes it difficult to book well in advance, but it is rarely a problem to find a room.

Hotels

In the recommendations below, price approximations for a double room per night are as follows:

€€€€ = over €300
€€€ = €200–300
€€ = €100–200
€ = under €100

€€€€

Amigo, 1–3 Rue de l'Amigo, tel: 02 547 4747; fax: 02 513 5277; e-mail: hotelamigo@hotelamigo.com; www.roccoforte hotels.com. Brussels' finest 5-start hotel has been totally refurbished by the Rocco Forte hotel group. Still a favourite with politicians, visiting actors and artists, it is as centrally located as it gets, just behind the Town Hall and the Grand' Place. The rooms are elegantly furnished in understated modern style.

Astoria, 103 Rue Royale, tel: 02 227 0505; fax: 02 217 1150; e-mail: H1154@accor-hotels.com; www.sofitel.com. The 19th-century Astoria Hotel was orig-inally intended to receive royal visi-tors. Today the rooms have been mod-ernised and have lost some of their character, but the chandeliers, mould-ings and palm trees are still in place, as they were when the likes of Sal-vador Dalí and the Aga Khan came to stay.

Château du Lac, 87 Avenue du Lac, Genval, tel: 02 655 7111; fax: 02 655 7444; e-mail: cdl@martins-hotels.com; www.martins-hotels.com. On the shore of the small but pretty Lac de Genval just outside Brussels, the château dates from the 1890s and is a copy of an old abbey. Genval is popular for walks.

Conrad International, 71 Avenue Louise, tel: 02 542 4242; fax: 02 542 4200; e-mail: brusselsinfo@conradhotels.com; www.conradhotels.com. A fine modern hotel, well positioned near the best shopping area, with a grand lobby and luxurious rooms.

Hilton Brussels, 38 Boulevard de Waterloo, tel: 02 504 1111; fax: 02 504 2111; e-mail: roomservations.brussels@ hilton.com; www.hilton.com. Prestigious hotel conveniently located near the upmar-ket shops and the Sablon area. Most rooms command great views over the city. A good brunch is served every Sunday.

Métropole, 31 Place de Brouckère, tel: 02 217 2300; fax: 02 218 0220; e-mail: info@metropolehotel.be; www.metropole-hotel.com. The Hôtel Métropole, from the Belle Epoque period, has an imposing facade embellished with caryatids, its grand art-nouveau inte-rior filled with plenty of polished teak, marble and symbolist stained glass windows. The cosy rooms are well equipped. An excellent breakfast is served under the palm-trees in the ele-gant Palm Court. Very good value at weekends.

Montgomery, 134 Avenue de Tervuren, tel: 02 741 8511; fax: 02 741 8500; e-mail: hotel@montgomery.be; www.montgomery.be. Splendid modern hotel with sumptuous rooms furnished in antique style-furniture with a fax and video in each room. Near the Parc du Cinquantenaire.

Radisson SAS, 47 Rue du Fossé-aux-Loups, tel: 02 219 2828; fax: 02 219 6262; e-mail: info.brussels@radissonsas.com; www.radissonsas.com. One of the city centre's finest luxury hotels, the SAS has earned a reputation for excellent service. Its facilities include airline check-in, a health suite, the top-class Sea Grill seafood restaurant, and a 'walk-in' cigar humidor.

€€€

Carrefour de l'Europe, 110 Rue du Marché-aux-Herbes, tel: 02 504 9400; fax: 02 504 9500; e-mail: info@carrefour europe.net; www.carrefoureurope.net. A comfortable modern hotel with a great city-centre location opposite the Place de l'Agora. The architecture is in harmony with the Flemish Renaissance surroundings.

Comfort Art Hotel Siru, 1 Place Rogier, tel: 02 203 3580; fax: 02 203 3303; e-mail: art.hotel.siru@skynet.be; www.comforthotelsiru.com. All rooms have been decorated by Belgian artists and each floor is dedicated to a famous poet, while the corridors are decorated with comic strips.

Le Dixseptième, 25 Rue de la Madeleine, tel: 02 502 5744; fax: 02 502 6424; e-mail: info@ledixseptieme.be; www.ledixseptieme.be. An intimate, smaller hotel, rare in Brussels, in the former residence of the Spanish ambassador, with 17 stylishly-furnished rooms.

Manos Premier, 100 Chaussée de Charleroi, tel: 02 537 9682; fax: 02 539 3655; e-mail: manos@manoshotel.com; www.manoshotel.com. A mansion-style hotel in the Avenue Louise area,

Manos aims to offer a more personalised service than the business-oriented chains.

Mayfair, 381–3 Avenue Louise, tel: 02 649 9800; fax: 02 649 2249; e-mail: mayfair@arcadis.be. Elegant hotel with cosy rooms furnished in British country style.

Royal Windsor, 5 Rue Duquesnoy, tel: 02 505 5555; fax: 02 505 5500; www.royalwindsorbrussels.com. A modern hotel with an old-fashioned sense of style and a location near the Grand' Place. Interesting variety of weekend packages.

Sablon, 2–4 Rue de la Paille, tel: 02 513 6040; fax: 02 514 8141; e-mail: info@hotellesablon.be; www.hotellesablon.be. A modern hotel with little character but situated near the antique shops of the Sablon area.

Saint Michel, 15 Grand' Place, tel: 02 511 0956; fax: 02 511 4600; e-mail: hotelsaintmichel@accueiletraditiongrandplace.be; www.accueiletraditiongrandplace.be. Dilapidated interior behind a splendid facade, but this is the only hotel on the square and the views are worth the slight discomfort.

€€

Agenda Louise, 6 Rue de Florence, tel: 02 539 0031; fax: 02 539 0063; e-mail: louise@hotel-agenda.com; www.hotel-agenda.com. Cosy rooms and friendly service in the vicinity of the shopping area around the avenue Louise make this a popular choice.

Argus, 6 Rue Capitaine Crespel, tel: 02 514 0770; fax: 02 514 1222; e-mail: reception@hotel-argus.be; www.hotel-argus.be. Good-value rooms in this small hotel in the avenue Louise area.

Arlequin, 17–19 Rue de la Fourche, tel: 02 514 1615; fax: 02 514 2202; e-mail: reservation@arlequin.be; www.arlequin.be. Small friendly hotel with comfortable rooms, some with views of the Grand' Place.

Bristol Stéphanie, 91 Avenue Louise, tel: 02 543 3311; fax: 02 538 0307; www.bristol.be. An ultra-modern hotel with an indoor swimming pool in the fashionable Avenue Louise shopping district. Great bargains at weekends.

Congrès, 42 Rue du Congrès, tel: 02 217 1890; fax: 02 217 1897; e-mail: info@hotelducongres.be; www.hotelducongres.be. Very welcoming hotel converted from two 19th-century maisons de maître.

Ibis Brussels off Grand' Place, 100 Rue du Marché-aux-Herbes, tel: 02 514 4040; fax: 02 514 5067; e-mail: H1046-RE@accor-hotels.com; www.ibishotel.com. A modern hotel that makes up for its lack of character with its reliability and a prime location a stone's throw from the Grand' Place.

Kasteel Gravenhof, 676 Alsembergsesteenweg, Dworp, tel: 02 380 4499; fax: 02 380 4060; e-mail: info@gravenhof.be; www.gravenhof.be. The nearest thing Brussels has to a Spanish-style *parador*, Gravenhof is an old Flemish-style château with a good restaurant, located 12km (7 miles) south of the city.

La Légende, 35 Rue du Lombard, tel: 02 512 8290; fax: 02 512 3493; e-mail: inf@hotellalegende.com; www.hotellalegende.com.

Looking down over the rooftops of Brussels

Pleasant hotel near the Grand' Place and Manneken-Pis with comfortable rooms around a quiet courtyard.

La Madeleine, 22 Rue de la Montagne, tel: 02 513 2973; fax: 02 502 1350; e-mail: hotel-la-madeleine@hotel-la-madeleine.be; www.hotel-la-madeleine.be. Excellent smaller hotel near the Grand' Place.

Queen Anne, 110 Boulevard Emile Jacqmain, tel: 02 217 1600; fax: 02 217 1838. In an area of Brussels that's looking up after years of decline, the Queen Anne is oriented towards business travellers. Its location is just far enough from the main centre to be slightly inconvenient, but in compensation it's relatively quiet.

Sabina, 78 Rue du Nord, tel: 02 218 2637; fax: 02 219 3239; e-mail: info@hotelsabina.be; www.hotelsabina.be. Converted 1920s town house in a quiet street near the inner ring road, and a 10- to 15-minute walk from the centre.

Welcome, 23 Quai au Bois-à-Brûler, tel: 02 219 9546; fax: 02 217 1887; e-mail: info@hotelwelcome.com; www.hotelwelcome.com. A small wonder, with 17 rooms, that's like a country auberge in the heart of town. Its enthusiastic and friendly owners fuss proudly around it and their guests. On the ground floor is their excellent fish and seafood restaunt, La Truite d'Argent

Windsor, 13 Place Rouppe, tel: 02 511 2014; fax: 02 514 0942; e-mail: info@hotel-windsor.com; www.hotel-windsor.com. Clean rooms on this central but quiet square between the Grand' Place and the Gare du Midi.

€

De Boeck's, 40 Rue Veydt, tel: 02 537 4033; fax: 02 534 4037; e-mail: hotel deboeck@skynet.be. Big rooms and reasonable rates at this hotel in a fine location off Avenue Louise make this an excellent choice for budget group travellers.

Les Bluets, 124 Rue Berckmans, tel: 02 534 3983; fax: 02 543 0970; e-mail: bluets@swing.be; www.belge.net/bluets. A small and friendly hotel in a beautiful building from 1864, with unusually and tastefully decorated rooms, located in a quiet street near Avenue Louise.

GUESTHOUSES

Duke of Windsor, 4 Rue Capouille, tel: 02 539 1819. Five comfortable rooms (non-smoking only) near Porte Louise.

Père Boudart, 592 Chaussée Romaine, 1853 Strombeek, tel: 02 460 7496; fax: 02 460 7816. Attractive guesthouse in the vicinity of the Heysel and the Parc de Laeken.

Rembrandt, 42 Rue de la Concorde, tel: 02 512 7139; fax: 02 511 7136. Guesthouse near Avenue Louise with high ceilings and an excellent Belgian breakfast.

BED AND BREAKFAST

For information on staying with local families, contact the following:

Bed & Breakfast Taxistop, 28 Rue du Fossé-aux-Loups, 1000 Brussels, tel: 070 222 292; fax: 223 2232; e-mail: bnb@taxistop.be; www.taxistop.be.

Bed & Brussels, 9 Rue Kindermans, 1050 Brussels, tel: 646 0737; fax:

644 0114; e-mail: info@bnb-brussels.be; www.bnb-brussels.

The Belgian Tourist Office produces the useful brochure, Bed and Breakfast: Benelux Guide, available from most tourist offices in Belgium and abroad.

YOUTH AND STUDENT ACCOMMODATION

Jeugdherberg Brueghel, 2 Rue du Saint Esprit, tel: 02 511 0436; fax: 02 512 0711; e-mail: brussel@vjh.be; www.vjh.be. Close to Gare Centrale; parking for bikes and motorbikes.

Centre Vincent van Gogh (CHAB), 8 Rue Traversière, tel: 02 217 0158; fax: 02 219 7995; e-mail: chab@ping.be; www.ping.be/chab. Large hostel, with 24-hour access.

Auberge de Jeunesse Jacques Brel, 30 Rue de la Sablonnière, tel: 02 218 0187; fax: 02 217 2005; e-mail: brussels. brel@laj.be; www.laj.be. Wide range of facilities.

Auberge de Jeunesse Génération Europe, 4 Rue de l'Eléphant, tel: 02 410 3858; fax: 02 410 3905; e-mail: brussels.europe@laj.be; www.laj.be. Located lightly out of town, but offers good facilities.

Sleep Well, 23 Rue du Damier, tel: 02 218 5050; fax: 02 218 1313; e-mail: info@sleepwell.be; www.sleepwell.be. Central location, Internet café, disabled access.

CAMPSITES

There are no campsites in Brussels itself. The nearest ones within reach of the city by public transport are:

Camping Welcome, 104 Kouterstraat, 3090 Overijse, tel: 02 687 7577 (open April–October only).

Camping Paul Charles, 114 Avenue Albert 1er, 1332 Genval, tel: 02 653 6215.

Camping de Renipoint, 7A Rue du Ry Beau Ry, 1380 Ohain (near Waterloo), tel: 02 654 0670.

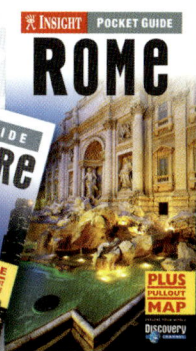

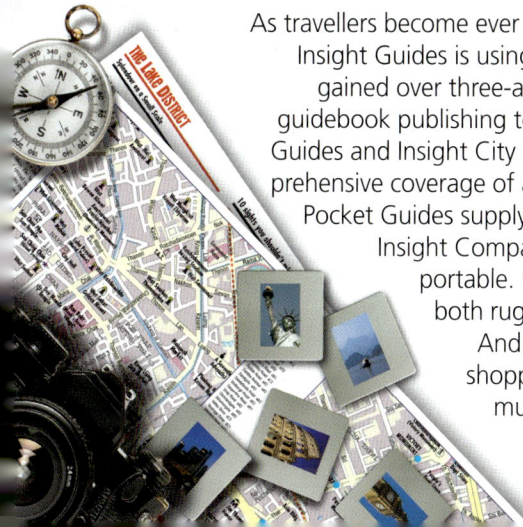

INDEX